A Learning Ideabook™

Native American Crafts Workshop

by Bonnie Bernstein and Leigh Blair

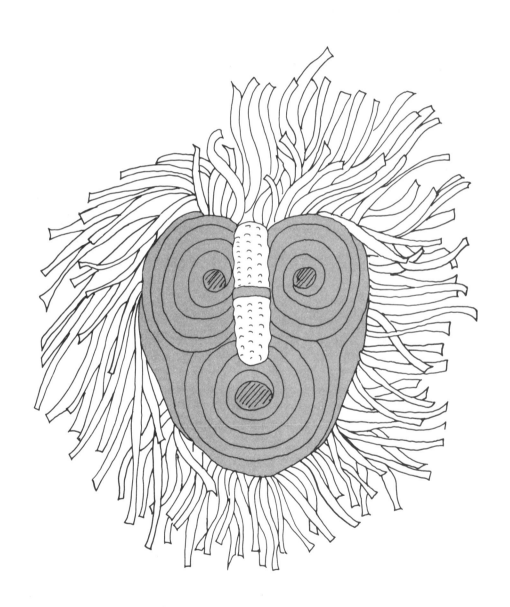

Fearon Teacher Aids, Carthage, Illinois

OTHER TITLES IN THE CRAFTS WORKSHOP SERIES:

INVENTORS WORKSHOP
MAKE YOUR OWN GAMES WORKSHOP
NATURE CRAFTS WORKSHOP
TRASH ARTISTS WORKSHOP

Designer: Jane Mitchell
Illustrator: Jaclyne Scardova
Cover designer: William Nagel

Entire contents copyright © 1982 by Fearon Teacher Aids,
1204 Buchanan Street, P.O. Box 280, Carthage, Illinois 62321.
Permission is hereby granted to reproduce the materials in
this book for noncommercial classroom use.

ISBN-0-8224-9784-0
Library of Congress Catalog Card Number: 81-82041
Printed in the United States of America.

1.9 8 7 6 5

Contents

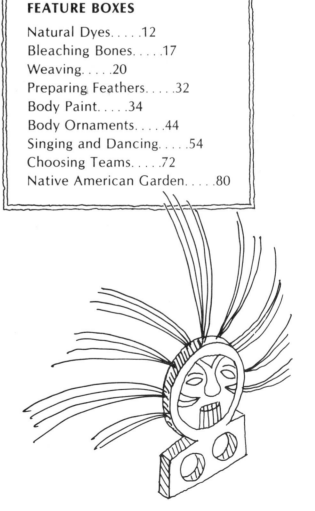

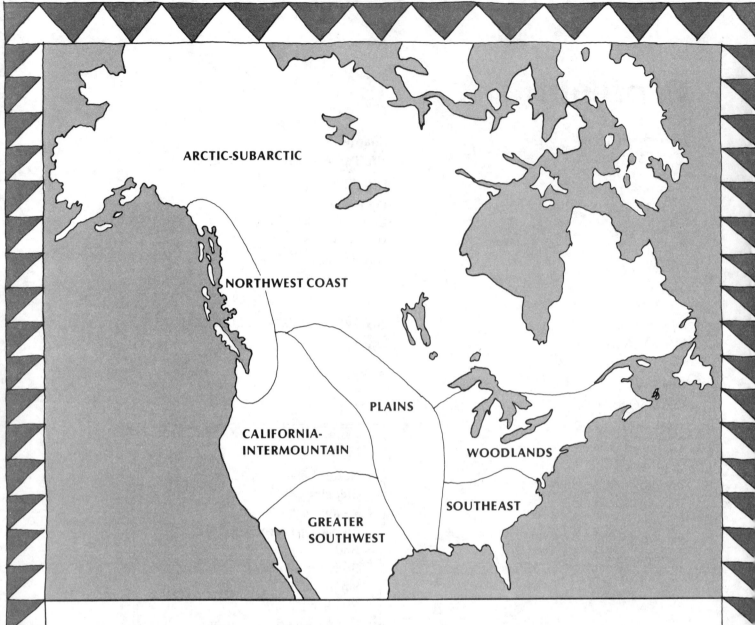

ARCTIC-SUBARCTIC

NORTHWEST COAST

PLAINS

CALIFORNIA-INTERMOUNTAIN

WOODLANDS

SOUTHEAST

GREATER SOUTHWEST

CULTURE AREAS OF NATIVE AMERICANS

Arctic-Subarctic

Aleut
Chippewa
Eskimo
Ojibwa

Northwest Coast

Chilkat
Chinook
Haida
Kwakiutl
Makah

Plains

Arapaho
Blackfoot
Cheyenne
Cree
Mandan
Pawnee
Sioux

California-Intermountain

Chumash
Hupa
Mission
Nez Perce
Paiute
Pomo
Salish
Ute

Greater Southwest

Acoma
Apache
Cora
Hopi
Huichol
Navaho
Pima
Pueblo
Yaqui
Zuni

Woodlands

Algonquin
Delaware
Iroquois
Menomini
Penobscot
Tuscarora

Southeast

Cherokee
Chickasaw
Choctaw
Creek
Seminole

Introduction

Behold, my brothers, the spring has come; the earth has received the embraces of the sun and we shall soon see the results of that love! Every seed is awakened and so has all animal life. It is through this mysterious power that we, too, have our being, and we therefore yield to our neighbors, even our animal neighbors, the same right as ourselves, to inhabit the land.

Sitting Bull, 1877

Native Americans believed that the spirit of the gods filled everything in nature. For this reason, they lived in harmony with their environment, treating with care and respect the plants, animals, and natural resources. They considered all things as sacred gifts, however ordinary or plentiful. Preserving the balance of nature was a way of living well on the earth.

By making Native American crafts firsthand, kids can learn a lot about the many different cultures which shared this deep gratitude for the earth and its generous provisions. Kids can learn how Native Americans lived, what they believed, how they worked, how they played, and what they used from their environment for food and crafts materials. A game mimicking the harpooning of a seal, for example, teaches basic hunting methods in the frozen Arctic. The rain symbols frequently painted on Pueblo pots, gourd rattles, and groaning sticks suggest the importance of water in the dry Southwest. Ceremonial offerings and effigies show the way Native Americans communicated with their gods.

Most importantly, the ancient wisdom of Native Americans can teach kids to rediscover their own environments. The experience of finding available materials and crafting them into useful items will help kids expand their awareness of the gifts of nature outside their own front doors. They will begin to notice the plants and grasses that can be made into a coil-wrap basket or eaten in a native salad. They will find that discarded husks from fresh corn on the cob are useful fibers for weaving an Iroquois medicine mask or making a Zuni shuttlecock.

Native Americans were very inventive about using the materials that nature provided, and they were always willing to experiment with new ones. If trade with outsiders brought new tools or materials that would make work easier or save time, those tools and materials were readily put to use. For example, groups throughout the Woodlands and Plains regions substituted European glass beads for dyed porcupine quills to embroider leather. Jewelry making flourished in the Greater Southwest as the cultures there learned skills of silversmithing from the Spaniards. And all native groups replaced stone and bone implements with precision metal tools.

The crafts projects in this book are authentic, or almost authentic, versions of items made in North America by Native Americans before 1900. By "almost authentic" we mean that we have introduced substitute materials, tools, or alternate steps to make some projects more practical for kids in the classroom or at home. Each project features a description of how the item was used or how it was meaningful to Native Americans in one or more culture areas. This explanation is followed by a list of materials and step-by-step directions and illustrations. Finally, there are suggestions for holding a Native American celebration as an appropriate occasion to play native instruments, perform native dances, prepare native foods, display native crafts, and play native games.

Native Americans believed that each person had a unique and separate path to follow on earth. This philosophy influenced their craftwork. Although there were traditional designs and patterns, every individual interpreted them a little differently. So, no two pottery bowls or ghost shirts were ever exactly alike. Although we provide some samples of Native American art and designs, and suggest the use of particular symbols and colors, we also encourage self-expression. Kids' craftwork should be as individual and creative as the craftwork of Native Americans.

CULTURE AREAS

Anthropologists divide native North America into culture areas to help organize their study of the great diversity of Native American life-styles. These culture areas reflect shared customs, available natural materials, similar economies, and other common characteristics. But there are almost as many differences as similarities among the various groups in an area. In *Native American Crafts Workshop*, we refer to these culture areas as shown on the map: Arctic and Subarctic, Northwest Coast, Great Plains, Woodlands, Southeast, California and Intermountain, and Greater Southwest. The sketches of these culture areas that follow are very general; they're for background information only. By using the Resources on pages 91–92, you can study individual Native American cultures and groups in greater detail for a more thorough and accurate understanding of them.

Arctic and Subarctic: Many months of heavy snowfall and severe cold made farming impossible in this area. Near the coast, groups hunted sea mammals such as walrus, seals, and whales. In the interior regions of tundra and thick forests, seasonal gathering of plant foods supplemented the hunting of caribou, elk, and moose. The most available crafts materials were bone, reindeer horn, animal skins, ivory tusks, bark, wood, and stone. During the long winter months there was ample time to carve tools and decorative items with imaginative and elaborate designs.

Northwest Coast: Salmon, seal, and sea otter were plentiful in the waters of this temperate region. Game such as deer, elk, bear, moose, and small fur animals were also abundant. The crafts materials most commonly used were shells, skins, ivory tusks, plant fibers, and wood. Impressive totem poles and masks were carved out of wood, and people used wooden containers instead of pottery. They wove animal hair and shredded bark into garments and blankets, and reeds and other grasses into baskets.

Great Plains: Native peoples here rapidly adopted the use of the gun and horse, introduced by Europeans. They hunted over great distances, following herds of buffalo. Extreme temperatures—hot summers and very cold winters—made farming very difficult. Along major rivers, a few groups grew corn, squash, and beans. Buffalo hides were made into clothing, tipis, and storage containers, and decorated with dyed porcupine quills or beads. Feathers were used decoratively and symbolically on ceremonial costumes.

Woodlands: Hunting and fishing were important around the freshwater lakes and along the Atlantic coast. Native groups farmed corn, squash, and beans where the growing season was long enough. The crafts materials included shells, skins, plant fibers, wood, and bark. Although some people made pottery, most preferred bark containers for carrying and storing things. Porcupine quills, moosehair, and beads were used for decoration.

Southeast: Native people here were skilled farmers, planting year-round in the rich valleys. They also hunted the many small game animals of the forests. Crafts materials included shells, feathers, plant fibers, and clay. A unique pottery was made of clay reinforced with shells and plant materials.

California and Intermountain: Game was scarce in these dry regions. Most groups depended on gathering roots, acorns, or seeds for food. Along the coast, people also gathered shellfish and caught fish. Weaving baskets out of plant fibers was the most highly developed craft, and beautiful featherwork decorated baskets and ceremonial costumes. Other crafts materials included shells and the skins and furs of small animals.

Greater Southwest: In this area's hot and dry climate, each year's farm crops survived only if the rains came. People guarded against years of drought by storing dried corn. They developed pottery making and blanket weaving as fine arts. They were the only native weavers in North America to use the loom. The craft materials commonly used were clay, plant fibers, wool, wood, and feathers.

The dry climate has preserved more crafts in the Southwest than in other areas. Today, many Native Americans continue to live there and work in the traditional arts. For these reasons, the crafts of the Southwest are probably the best known and best represented of all Native American crafts today.

ASSEMBLING CRAFTS MATERIALS

In the natural world around them, Native Americans found a ready supply of materials to make clothing, tools, containers, shelters, musical instruments, and games. Kids can find most of the materials needed for *Native American Crafts Workshop* in their own environments—in the yard or park, at home or in school, or in local stores—without too much difficulty or expense.

Many of the crafts projects require materials common to most classrooms and homes—paints, wood scraps, clay, yarn, twine needle and thread, and so forth. Some of the projects also call for some unusual materials; although they aren't standard household items, they are readily available.

Below are detailed explanations of the materials Native Americans used, and suggestions for finding those materials or appropriate substitutes. Turn part of a room, a closet, or a shelf into a Native American workshop and start hunting and gathering crafts materials. Try to be as creative about using and reusing materials as Native Americans were.

Materials from Animals: Native Americans saved the bones, antlers, skins, and horns from animals killed for food. They used as many parts of an animal as possible. For example, even the cheek hairs of moose were dyed and used as colorful thread for embroidering, braiding, and plaiting. Women stripped sinew from the muscles of deer and other game animals, then pulled it through their teeth to make fine fibers for thread and string. A splinter from a large animal's leg bone made a sturdy awl for punching holes through which to sew skins or bind coiled baskets. Most Native Americans relied on a digging stick for planting, but some also attached a large shoulder bone from a deer or moose to a stick for a hoe, or a set of antlers to a stick for a rake.

Bones: Ask a local butcher to save beef marrow bones from the leg or thigh. If the butcher is willing, have them cut to the specific sizes you need. Otherwise, cut them yourself with a small hacksaw; they're soft enough to cut easily. See Bleaching Bones, page 17, for directions on how to clean and prepare bones for crafting.

Leather scraps and thongs: Ask a local handbag maker or sandal maker to save some small scraps and thongs. Or buy a mixed bag of scraps at a hobby shop or through a mail-order catalog (see Resources, page 92).

Materials from Plants: Plants and plant parts were used by Native Americans for making cloth, weaving baskets, dyeing fibers, decorating, and painting. Bark from birch and other trees was used for containers, canoes, and roofs. The pointed tip of a yucca leaf with a strip of plant fiber still attached was probably the first self-threaded needle. Strong ropes were made from twisted hemp or milkweed fibers, and the pitch or resin from pine trees was used for waterproofing and gluing. Even thorns had a use: they were ready-made thumbtacks and pins.

From Native American gardens came more crafts materials. Dried gourds were made into containers, whistles, drums, bowls, and tools. Dried corncobs made handy corks, and the strong fibers of the cornhusks were used to braid, tie, and wrap.

Corn: Grow your own corn if possible (see Native American Garden, page 80). Or buy fresh corn on the cob in season and save the cob and husks after eating. Dry the husks flat in a well-aired spot if you're not using them immediately. Husks are also available in packages in some supermarkets. The cobs should be scraped clean, then dried overnight. In the fall, save the colorful kernels from dried "Indian corn" to use as beads, mosaic pieces, or game counters.

Gourds: If you have a garden, grow and dry your own *lagenaria* and ornamental gourds (see Native American Garden, page 80). Leave the gourds in a cool dry place for 6 to 8 weeks until the shells are hard and the seeds inside rattle. If you don't grow them, ask a local grower to save a few in season, or buy some unshellacked gourds at an ornamental florists' supply store.

Raffia: This is a useful fiber made from palm leaves. Crafts and hobby shops sell raffia by weight. Don't buy too much; a few ounces will be enough for the projects in this book.

Sticks: Pick up dried branches on the ground in a park or other wooded area. For more pliable wood, select a green branch and use a knife to cut it off at a joint. A pointed stick is a good tool for incising or scratching designs in clay, for punching holes, or for painting simple line designs. A pencil sharpener whittles a good point on a medium-size stick. For paintbrushes, Native Americans chewed the tip of a yucca leaf or a branch of a soap plant until the end was frayed, and then trimmed it. Find a stick that has a soft, fibrous tip. Make sure the stick comes from a tree or plant that you know is not poisonous. Chew it and trim it to make a paintbrush.

Materials from Birds: Feathers were the most important materials birds provided, though small wing bones were used as whistles. Sometimes a small area like the scalp or throat of a bird was used whole since the feathers were tiny and colorful. Tail feathers were used for fans and hair plumes and were strung together to decorate pipes and clothing. Wing feathers were made into fans and capes or were clipped and used as colorful pieces in feather mosaics. Small, unusual feathers, like the quail's plume, were woven into the rims of baskets. Long and springy hackle, or neck, feathers were attached to costumes and masks to add movement.

Feathers: Gather a supply of small, fluffy feathers and long, shafted feathers from a nearby park, pond, beach, zoo, birdfeeder, or local poultry farm. If you call ahead, a turkey or chicken ranch may save some feathers for you. Also, stop in at a few pet shops. They regularly clip their macaws, parrots, and cockatoos and may be willing to save the bright feathers.

See Preparing Feathers, page 32, for directions on how to clean and prepare feathers for crafting.

Materials from the Sea: Coastal people used many materials from the sea, but the very valuable or useful materials were traded widely and used by Native Americans across the continent. Strings of shells, such as dentalium and quahog, were standards of exchange in trade. Tools and body ornaments were carved from ivory tusks and teeth from large sea mammals and fish. Sharkskin made an excellent sandpaper, and cup-shaped fish vertebrae were used to hold small quantities of paint. Clam shells were used as ready-made tweezers for plucking out beard hair.

Shells: Collect an assortment of shells at the beach or buy them at a pet shop or an import store where they're sold as decorations. Small shells with holes bored through them by natural predators can be stitched to clothing or strung as neck ornaments. The notched edge of a shell was used by Native American pottery makers to create repeating patterns on the walls of clay vessels. Shells with interesting edges can be used to stamp designs on clay or cloth, or to apply body paint.

Materials from the Earth: Rocks, minerals, and soil were put to use by Native Americans everywhere. Grinding stones turned corn into meal and soft rocks into fine powders. Sandstone and pumice were used to smooth beads, wood, and bone. Rocks that contained silica, such as flint, chert, and obsidian, were chipped and shaped with harder rocks, to become sharp-edged tools and points for arrows. Colorful stones became jewelry or talismans, and copper was formed into small ornaments. Native Americans used clay soils to make bricks to build houses, and shaped it into sturdy pots and vessels.

Many of the earth's minerals color the soils. Native Americans used these minerals to color their crafts and paint their bodies. See Body Paint, page 34, for directions on how to prepare soils for body painting.

1

Crafts for Everyday Use

Native Americans crafted many articles for day-to-day use—clothing, containers in which to cook and carry food and water, and tools for hunting and farming. They gave these everyday items as much artistic care as the objects they crafted for ceremonial use. Everyday articles were usually decorated with abstract geometric designs; ceremonial objects were decorated with symbols that had special religious meanings.

In keeping with their overall religious beliefs, Native Americans were careful to respect the materials they used to make their everyday crafts. Some people sang to the plants as they pulled them from the ground. Others apologized to the animals they killed before skinning them.

Leather Pouch

Native Americans made small pouches from pieces of soft buckskin or small animal skins. The pouches carried personal valuables, such as small quantities of dry mineral paints, tobacco, or magical objects like pebbles.

Most warriors carried bags containing good luck charms to protect them from harm. In the Woodlands, warriors' pouches held tokens of victories in battle. In the Southeast, a group going off to war carried a decorated pouch holding a sacred rock crystal, used to predict their success or failure.

Other pouches contained rattles from a rattlesnake's tail, buffalo horns, claws, or animal effigies. The Blackfoot believed that a spirit helper, an animal or bird, told each person what sacred objects to gather to carry in a pouch. The Pawnee believed that a star guided people searching for such objects. If the contents of a pouch had powerful magic, they could give a person great status and success in fighting or healing.

The healers of the Winnebago carried an otter skin pouch filled with herbs, bark, feathers, and stones. According to myth, spirits carrying otters had brought a dead boy back to life; so the otter medicine bags had great power.

Sacred pouches were not always worn around the neck or on a belt. Sometimes they were hung in the dwelling or on a horse to keep them at hand.

MATERIALS

Square of chamois or other soft leather
(Chamois cloths can be purchased in the housewares or the auto maintenance department of most supermarkets and hardware and department stores.)
Pencil
Scissors
Hole punch
Leather thong about 1½ times as long as the chamois
Small beads (optional)
Needle (narrow enough to string beads) and thread (optional)
Acrylic or oil paints and brushes (optional)
Feathers (optional)

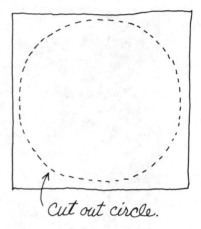

Cut out circle.

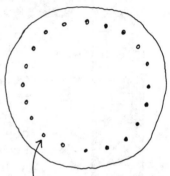

Punch holes 1" apart and 1" from the edge.

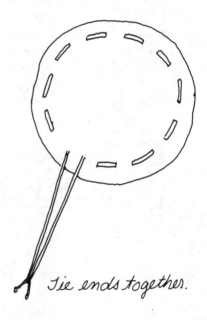

Tie ends together.

DIRECTIONS

1. Pencil a large circle on the chamois. Cut it out.
2. Mark an even number of dots about an inch from the edge of the chamois and about an inch apart, as shown.
3. Punch out the marked dots.
4. Thread the thong through the holes and then tie the ends together in a knot.
5. Decorate the bag with paint or with bead stitching. The Lazy Squaw beading stitch is shown in the illustration. Several small feathers can be tied onto the end of the thong (untie the knot first).
6. Gather up the pouch by pulling the thong ends. Then go on a search for special objects to put in it. Or grind some earth paints (see page 34) and make a pouch to store each color.

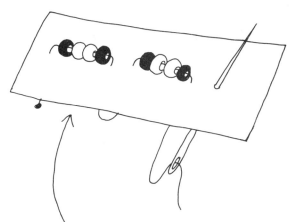

Example of Lazy Squaw stitch used to bead the pouch.

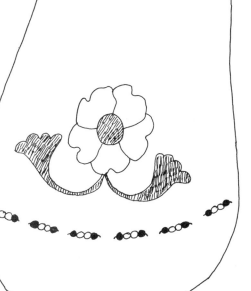

Coiled Basket

Basket makers sang special songs to the plants while they collected and prepared the fibers for weaving. They always worked with great care because baskets were so useful. Mothers carried babies on their backs in cradlelike baskets. Men and women wore cone-shaped baskets as backpacks to carry heavy loads of firewood, grain, or stones. Basket bowls, waterproofed with pitch, became water containers and cooking pots. Large woven jars stored grain; flat woven trays held seeds for roasting or were used to sift grains or carry food.

Some baskets were made for special occasions, like the Navaho coiled wedding basket. From this shallow basket, a bride and groom fed one another cornmeal and pollen and shared this sacred food with their wedding guests. The husband and wife kept the basket until one partner in the marriage died; then the other burned it.

The Pomo of California were probably the finest basket makers. Some of their baskets were made using the coil-wrap method. Bundles of grasses, reeds, or roots were wrapped with plant fiber and stitched together in a continuous coil. Binding the coils together with colored fibers produced geometric designs. The Pomo also decorated their ceremonial gift baskets with abalone shell, or wove in delicate feathers so that the baskets resembled the soft breasts of birds.

MATERIALS

Large roasting pan, 9 by 13 inches
Long, dried grasses or split reeds for core
    material (for example, yucca, cattail, tall
    weeds); a bundle about 6 inches in
    diameter
Raffia, about 1 ounce
Natural dyes and enameled pot (optional—
    see Natural Dyes, page 12)
Blunt tapestry needle
Dish towel
Scissors

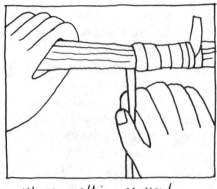

Wrap raffia around bundle.

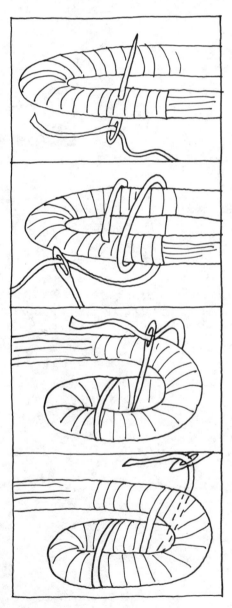

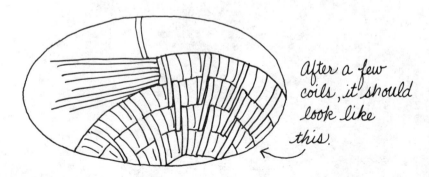

After a few coils, it should look like this.

10

DIRECTIONS

1. Fill the pan with warm water and soak the grasses or reeds for an hour or until they're supple.
2. Color the raffia with natural dyes if desired (see Natural Dyes on page 12).
3. Wet the raffia before threading and knotting it. Keep the raffia slightly damp by placing it in a wet towel while working. This will make it pull more smoothly through the coils.
4. Make a bundle about ¼ to ½ inch thick of the core material. Starting at one end of the bundle, take the damp piece of raffia and wrap it tightly around a 2½-to 3-inch length of the bundle, completely covering the core.
5. Bend the wrapped section in half. Push the needle through the core and bind the halves as shown. Use the same thread of raffia to both wrap and stitch.
6. Wrap another inch of the bundle. Then bend and curve this section around the center. Stitch over and under this coil as shown. Bring the raffia tightly up around the bundle. This will bind the new coil to the old one in a continuing spiral.
7. Keep wrapping the bundle inch by inch and stitching each inch to the coil beneath as in step 6. After you have several coils, begin stacking them before binding them—that is, build the basket up as well as out.
8. Add more core material to keep the spiral going. When the bundle is wrapped to about 1 inch from the end, jam a new bundle into the end. Try to keep the bundle the same thickness for even coils.
9. To begin using a new raffia thread, hold the old end down next to the bundle and wrap over it with the new thread. Wrap the new thread on itself several times to hold it in place.
10. Continue wrapping, coiling, and stitching until the basket is the size and shape you want. To finish, clip the bundle on an angle as shown. Overlap the raffia several times to bind the end to the last coil. Slip the needle under a wrap of raffia and snip off the thread close to the coil.

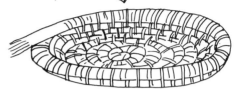

Start building coils upward. ↘

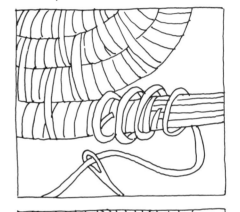

wrap new thread on itself several times as you wrap around the bundle.

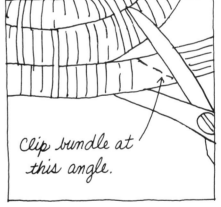

Clip bundle at this angle.

NATURAL DYES

Native Americans used plant materials to make beautiful, soft colors to dye wool, cotton, and other fibers. They made almost every color, though shades of yellow were the easiest to produce.

Listed below are some of the plants Native Americans used for coloring. Experiment making natural dyes with these or other plants in your environment. As a general rule, if the plant part is hard, like bark or sticks, pound or grind it to loosen the fibers; if it's soft, like flower petals or berries, use it as is.

Wash the plant material first. Then put it, ground up or whole, in a large enameled pot and fill the pot with water. (Metal pots may change the color, though sometimes that produces an interesting result.) Boil until the color is a little darker than you'd like. Strain the dye material out and add a little salt and baking soda to the colored water, or dyebath. For a more permanent dye, add a teaspoon of alum, available from a hardware or crafts store.

To dye wool or heavy cloth, soak it in warm water before putting it in the dyebath. Let it boil in the dyebath for about an hour and then let it cool in the pot. To dye raffia, thread, or thin cloth, soak them in the dyebath for several hours.

Rinse all dyed materials several times in cold water. Then hang them up to dry—away from direct sunlight or heat, which may cause bleaching.

Color	Plant Material	Color	Plant Material
Blacks	wild grapes, hickory bark, alder bark, dogwood bark, mountain mahogany bark	Purples	blueberries, raspberries, blackberries, rotten maple wood
Blues	larkspur petals, alfalfa flowers, sunflower seeds	Reds	sumac berries, dogwood bark, beets, cranberries
Browns	walnut shells, birch bark	Yellows	onion skins, goldenrod stems and flowers, sunflower petals, dock roots, marigold petals, moss, peach leaves, birch leaves, sagebrush
Greens	moss, algae, lily-of-the-valley leaves, juniper berries		

Calendar Stick

The Winnebago notched sticks as a way to record time and important events such as a meteor shower or the birth of a new family member. Notches on the front of the stick recorded the moons, or months. Notches on the side of the stick represented the winters, or years. Calendar sticks were handed down to family members through each generation.

Groups in the Plains recorded time and events by painting symbolic figures, or *pictographs,* on large animal skins. This kind of calendar was called a "winter count" (the new year began in winter) and might cover many years.

Different Native American groups began the year's count with different months, and divided the seasons at different times. Most measured days as suns, and nights as sleeps. The Zuni divided the year in half, leaving half the moons "named," and the other half "unnamed." The unnamed moons were known by symbolic colors. The year was called "the passage of time," the seasons the "steps," and the months the "crescents." Most Native Americans named their months or moons after some activity that took place during that time of the year. Others named them after animals or stars that appeared during the month.

MATERIALS

Long flat stick (like a paint stirrer or small
   garden stake)
Hammer and nail, or drill with ⅛-inch bit
Thong or cord, about 6 inches long
Poster paints and brushes

DIRECTIONS

1. Hammer a nail or drill a hole in the center at the top end of the stick. Slip the thong or cord through the hole and tie the ends.
2. Begin the calendar on the first of the year or on the day of an important event, such as the arrival of a new baby or your birthday. The Winnebago made their first notch at the sound of the first thunder in the autumn. Record the time or occasion with marks and picture symbols.
3. Hang the calendar stick on a hook or a nail in a place where you can get at it easily. Continue to record moons from month to month, and make a special symbol for every special occasion during the count. Include family events so that many winters from now, when you bring out the calendar stick, the picture record will be a "scrapbook" of events.

Clay Coiled Pot

Although people in other areas made pottery, the Greater Southwest was, and still is, best known for this Native American craft. Pueblo peoples used clay pots to store, prepare, and serve food; to carry and store water; and to hold ceremonial offerings such as cornmeal. (The Woodlands people relied more on birch bark containers, and the Northwest Coast and California groups preferred wooden bowls and woven baskets for most of these same uses.)

All the Pueblo groups used the coiling method to make pots, but each group had its own characteristic designs and decorations. Because the people depended so much on rain for their livelihood, they often painted cloud symbols on the pottery. Other common designs were lines and shapes, squash blossoms, birds, animals, and Kachinas. Pottery from the Santo Domingo Pueblo always had a small gap in the lines painted around a pot. This gap was the "spirit path." The people believed that every vessel contained a spirit that would sometimes leave and return again. If a path were not left open, the spirit might break the pot trying to get out.

MATERIALS

Soft brush
Clay, self-hardening
Piece of gourd or shell for smoothing
Sharp stick, piece of corncob, scallop shell,
  or string for texturing (optional)
Poster paints and brushes

DIRECTIONS

1. Pull off a small lump of clay and press it into a round, flat base about ½ inch thick. Roughen the top edge. Use a brush dipped in water to moisten the top.
2. Pull off a larger lump. Roll it into a rope about ½ inch in diameter. Coil this rope around the flat base. Use your fingers to press the coil into the roughened surface of the base. Join the coil and base by smoothing the clay together.
3. Make another rope of clay. Coil it around the pot on top of the first one.
4. After you have coiled a rope of clay around the pot, pinch and shape it into a rough wall before adding the next rope. Do this by holding one hand against the inside of the pot to support the wall while shaping the outside of the pot with your finger at the same spot. Try to keep the walls of the pot the same thickness.

Jar filled with water

always roughen the surface of the clay and moisten it slightly with water before joining 2 pieces of clay.

Roll clay into a rope.

Join the coil and base together by smoothing the clay together.

5. Continue adding ropes of clay, stacking them in coils, and shaping them upward and outward until the pot is the height and width you want. Rub the surface smooth with a smooth rock, a shell, or the back of a spoon.

6. The clay must be moist if the walls are to be textured. Use a scallop shell, a piece of corncob, or string pressed into the soft clay to produce an interesting texture. To incise, or scratch, a design on the walls of the pot, allow the pot to dry a while. When it is firm but still damp, incise the walls with a sharp stick or similar tool.

7. Allow the pot to dry slowly in a cool place. It will be lighter-colored and hard. Depending on the clay, this will take several days to dry thoroughly.

8. Paint the pot with geometric designs or symbols (see Native American Designs and Colors, pages 86–90). Paint the outside and also the inside of the pot. For some Native Americans, the most important part of the design was on the inside of the pot.

Note: Pots made this way (without baking them) are good containers for dry things, but they will not hold liquids.

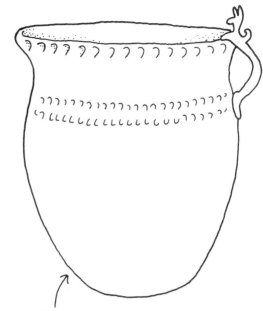

Pot with a textured surface. Fashion animal shapes and attach as handles or decoration.

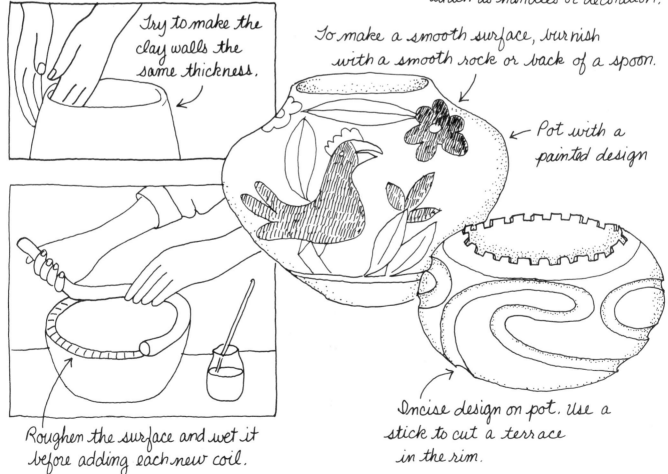

Try to make the clay walls the same thickness.

To make a smooth surface, burnish with a smooth rock or back of a spoon.

← Pot with a painted design

Roughen the surface and wet it before adding each new coil.

Incise design on pot. Use a stick to cut a terrace in the rim.

15

Possession Stick

Native Americans identified what belonged to them in many artistic ways. Along the Northwest Coast, families carved and erected tall totem poles in front of their dwellings bearing all the symbols of the family's heritage. They used animal symbols because the deeds of a clan were linked with miracles and heroic acts performed by animals in mythology. The totem pole was essentially a family history, and since each pole featured a unique set of symbols, it was also a means of identification, just like a family name.

Arrows, too, were decorated uniquely by their owners. After a successful hunt, all the dead animals were laid out together. A woman could identify which animal to skin by the unique pattern of colored stripes on her husband's arrow, which was left in the animal's flesh.

When gathering firewood in the forests, Native Americans would stake a possession stick—a shaft with one or more decorated crossbars—near their own piles. This marker identified the wood as belonging to a particular family, and no person outside that family would touch or take it.

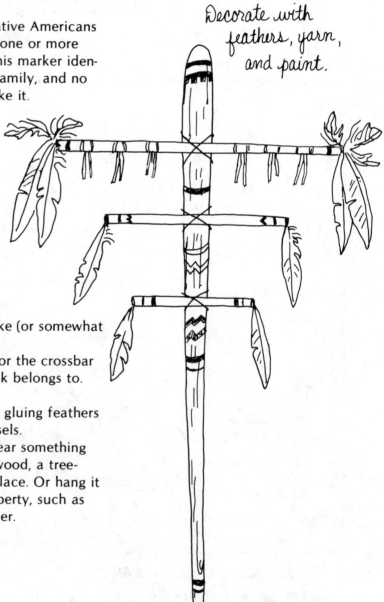

Decorate with feathers, yarn, and paint.

MATERIALS

Strong cord, about 12 inches
Small stake or sturdy stick
Shorter stick for crossbar
Acrylic paints and brushes
Feathers or colored yarn (optional)

DIRECTIONS

1. Use cord to bind the short stick to the stake (or somewhat larger stick) in a *T* as shown.
2. Paint colored marks along the main shaft or the crossbar that will identify whom the possession stick belongs to. Use personal symbols and colors.
3. The crossbar can be decorated by tying or gluing feathers to the ends or by adding colorful yarn tassels.
4. Place the possession stick in the ground near something that belongs to you—a pile of family firewood, a treehouse or club house, a garden, a private place. Or hang it up on something you consider private property, such as the door to your room or your school locker.

BLEACHING BONES

Native Americans cleaned animal bones by leaving them on an anthill for a few days or by boiling them and laying them in the sun to bleach.

It's quicker to scrape the sides and poke out the raw marrow in the middle of the bone with a knife or skewer than to let the ants eat it out. After most of the marrow is out, the bones are ready to be boiled and bleached. Set some object like a piece of sponge in the bottom of a pot. This will prevent the bones from resting on the bottom and possibly discoloring where they touch the pot. Put the bones in the pot and cover them with water. Add a little bleach or lemon juice to make them whiter. Then boil the bones for about an hour.

Native Americans sanded their bones with sandstone or pumice. Try using a medium coarse sandpaper to rub the bone smooth. To sand the interior, wrap the sandpaper around a pencil and work it around the inside. For a polish, squeeze some toothpaste onto a cloth and rub it onto the surface of the bone. The best polish of all is years of good use and handling.

Needle Case

On winter hunting trips in the Arctic, the Eskimo brought along a needle case containing a sewing kit. Temperatures averaged 20°F below freezing in winter, and a kit to make repairs in torn clothing could mean the difference between life and death.

For warmth, the Eskimo made their hunting outfits out of two suits of caribou skins sewn together; one had fur on the outside and the other had the fur on the inside. A hunter also wore a hood, mittens, boots with sealhide soles, and a wooden visor or goggles to protect the hunter's eyes from the bright snow.

Needle cases actually held an awl made of bone or ivory. The awl was used to punch holes in the skins so that a strand of sinew stripped from the leg muscle of a reindeer could be threaded through. (The kind of needle and thread used with cloth wouldn't work on clothing made of tough hides.) Awls were valuable. They were stored in the needle cases to protect them from loss or damage.

The sewing kit also included a bone creaser to press down the bulky seams and a sealskin thimble to help push the awl through. The cases themselves were usually made out of walrus tusks. They were carved with geometric shapes or animal symbols and then rubbed with hematite, a brownish-red mineral, to color in the grooves of the design.

MATERIALS

Pencil
Bleached marrow bone, 4 to 7 inches long
  (see Bleaching Bones, page 17)
Black or red poster paint and brush
Acrylic sealer spray
Tongue depressor
Ruler
Matte knife or awl
2 leather thongs, each 2 inches
  longer than the bone
Soft leather scrap, about
  1 by 3 inches
Tapestry or darning needle
2 stiff leather scraps, about
  2 by 3 inches each
Scissors
White glue

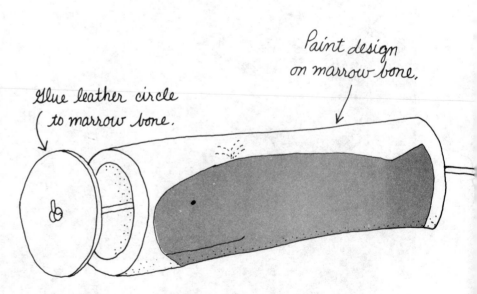

Glue leather circle to marrow bone.

Paint design on marrow bone.

DIRECTIONS

1. Lightly pencil a design on the marrow bone. Traditional Eskimo designs were geometric patterns or animal symbols (see Native American Designs and Colors, page 86–90). Paint the lines. After the paint dries, spray the bone with acrylic sealer to protect and polish the design.

2. Use a ruler to mark off inches and half-inches on one edge of the tongue depressor. Paint the marks.

3. About ½ inch from each end of the tongue depressor, rotate the tip of a knife or use an awl to make a hole. Slip a thong through each hole and tie a knot. The depressor is now a combination seam creaser and ruler.

4. Take the soft leather scrap and cut a small slit at each end. Slip the end of one thong from the depressor up through one slit and down through the other. Stick a needle in the middle of the leather scrap. The scrap is now a needle holder.

5. Trace each end of the bone onto a stiff leather scrap and cut out the two circles with a matte knife or scissors. Make a small slit in the center of each.

6. Thread the string of tools through the bone case and attach them to the leather circles as shown, making a large knot on each end.

7. Glue one leather circle onto the end of the bone to close it off. The other circle is both a stopper (it keeps the other tools from sliding off the thong) and a flat palm thimble.

8. Wrap the needle holder around the depressor, and insert them both into the case for safekeeping. All tools but the stopper should be stored inside the needle case. The stopper rests flat on top like a loose cap.

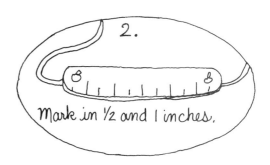

Mark in ½ and 1 inches.

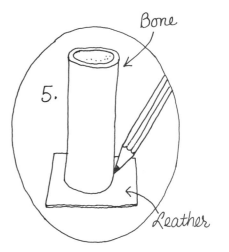

Bone

5.

Leather

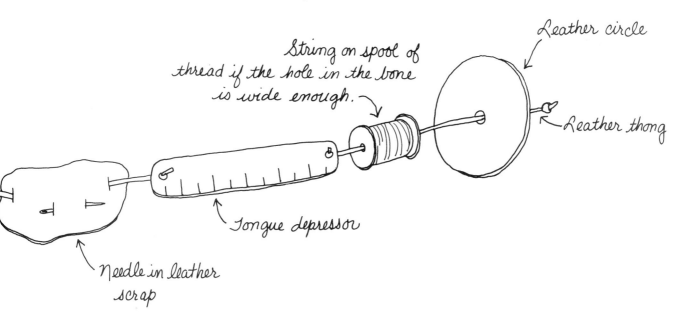

String on spool of thread if the hole in the bone is wide enough.

Leather circle

Leather thong

Tongue depressor

Needle in leather scrap

WEAVING

Native Americans in the Southwest believed that the Spider People, characters in mythology who caught rain clouds in the webs they wove, taught the first people on earth how to weave.

Although other groups braided and twisted fibers by hand to make bags, belts, blankets, and sashes, the Southwestern groups were the only ones to use true looms. The loom separated every other fiber mechanically and made weaving much quicker.

Like other groups, the people of the Southwest originally wove fibers such as cotton, bark, and buffalo and goat hair. But after the Europeans introduced sheep, they were quick to adopt wool, which made strong, heavy yarn for warm clothing. The Navaho, in particular, became expert shepherds and wool weavers. Their blankets were striking— colored with soft, natural dyes and woven in seemingly perfect geometric patterns. But, in fact, Navaho women always wove a small mistake into the design of a rug or blanket, believing that if they were to succeed in making a perfect thing, their life on earth would be over.

The Southwestern groups used a variety of looms. The vertical looms on which they wove their large blankets and pieces of cloth were either free standing or suspended from the branch of a tree. The simplest loom was a belt or sash loom that strapped around the back of a weaver to keep the threads taut. Like other crafts in the Southwest, the fine art of weaving is still practiced today.

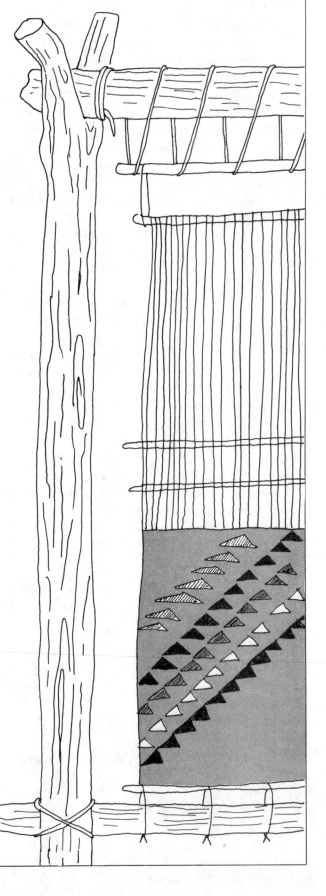

Eye Shade

The introduction of horses to the Plains changed life in many ways. The freedom to travel hundreds of miles on horseback in search of buffalo seemed to suit many native peoples more than farming. Because they were constantly moving their camps, the Plains people stopped making breakable goods, such as pottery, or crafts that required local materials, such as birch bark. Instead, they came to rely almost entirely on buffalo skins to make whatever they needed.

Hides were removed from the buffalo, then scraped, dried, and scraped again. Eventually, the clean, stiff rawhide was ready to use. Women were responsible for preparing hides and crafting them into articles such as *parfleches* (large envelopelike containers), trunks, pouches, cylinders for carrying rolled-up feather war bonnets, knife sheaths, buckets, dippers, cups, drumheads, rattles, shields, cradles, mortars for grinding food, and eye shades or visors to keep out the sun.

Most rawhide articles were brightly painted. Different peoples favored particular geometric patterns, combining squares, rectangles, and triangles. Although it was not common, individual artists sometimes included religious symbols in these designs.

MATERIALS

Pencil
Leather, sturdy piece about 9 by 12 inches
Scissors or matte knife
Tape measure
Oil or acrylic paints and brushes

DIRECTIONS

1. Pencil the pattern shown onto the back of the leather rectangle and cut it out.
2. Use a tape measure to measure around your head. Divide the measurement by 3. That will roughly be the diameter of your head. Draw a circle with this diameter on the leather as shown.
3. Draw a second circle within the first. This circle should be 1½ or 2 inches smaller than the first all around.
4. Cut out the smaller circle.
5. Scallop the edges of the circle by cutting in almost as far as the penciled larger circle as shown. Cut in about ½ inch short of the larger circle.

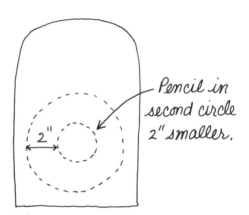

Front of visor

Pencil in a circle the diameter of your head.

use this pattern to cut visor out of 9" X 12" piece of leather.

Pencil in second circle 2" smaller.

2"

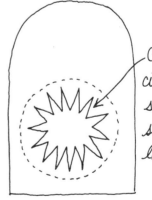

Cut center circle as shown. Cut ½" short of larger circle.

6. Try the eye shade on for size. If it's too tight, cut a little further into the scalloped circle. Keep in mind that the leather will stretch with wear.
7 Paint bright geometric designs on the eye shade in the traditional Plains colors—red, blue, yellow, black, and brown.

 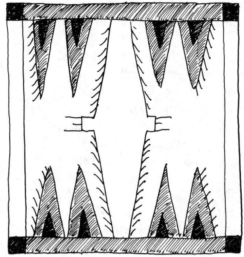 

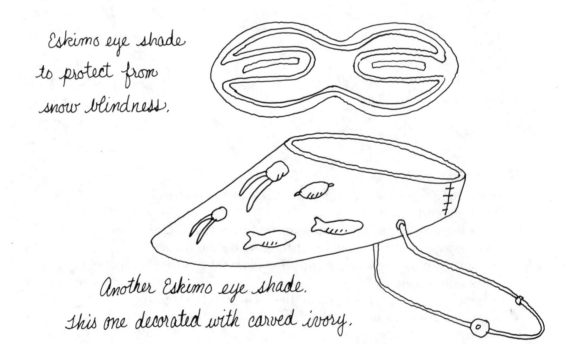

Eskimo eye shade to protect from snow blindness.

Another Eskimo eye shade. This one decorated with carved ivory.

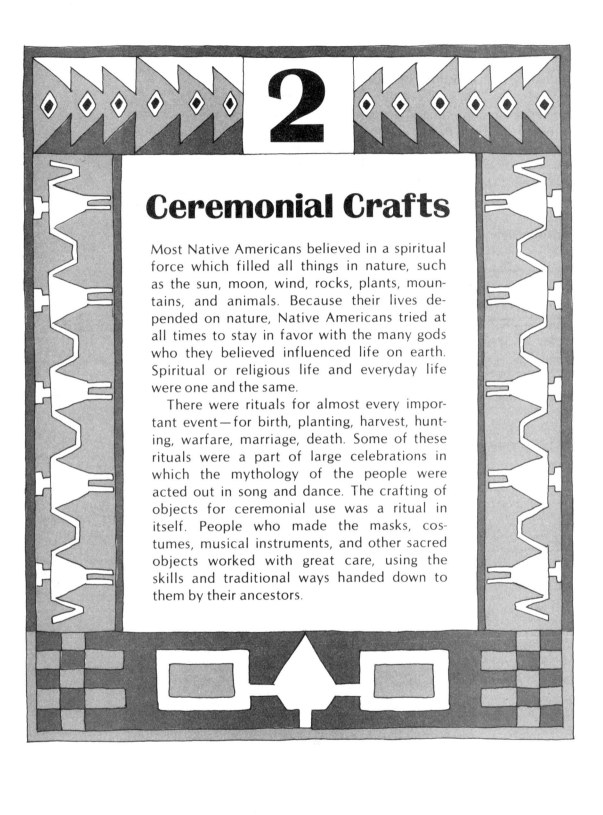

2

Ceremonial Crafts

Most Native Americans believed in a spiritual force which filled all things in nature, such as the sun, moon, wind, rocks, plants, mountains, and animals. Because their lives depended on nature, Native Americans tried at all times to stay in favor with the many gods who they believed influenced life on earth. Spiritual or religious life and everyday life were one and the same.

There were rituals for almost every important event—for birth, planting, harvest, hunting, warfare, marriage, death. Some of these rituals were a part of large celebrations in which the mythology of the people were acted out in song and dance. The crafting of objects for ceremonial use was a ritual in itself. People who made the masks, costumes, musical instruments, and other sacred objects worked with great care, using the skills and traditional ways handed down to them by their ancestors.

Finger Masks

The Eskimo held dances both for religious festivals and for social gatherings—especially during the long winter months. In these dances the Eskimo acted out many of the important aspects of their lives. Each dance had its own story, song, and gestures, and was often performed with intricate staging and props, such as trap doors or secret entrances and mechanical birds that "flew" across the stage of the dance igloo.

In many of the dances, men wore wooden face masks representing various characters of Eskimo religion and mythology. Masks of animals and bird spirits and of the sun and moon gods were very common. Women dancers wore very small versions of these masks on their fingers. Finger masks were small, carved pieces of wood decorated with feathers and fur. As the women danced, the feathers would wave with their swaying body movements and become a part of the dance.

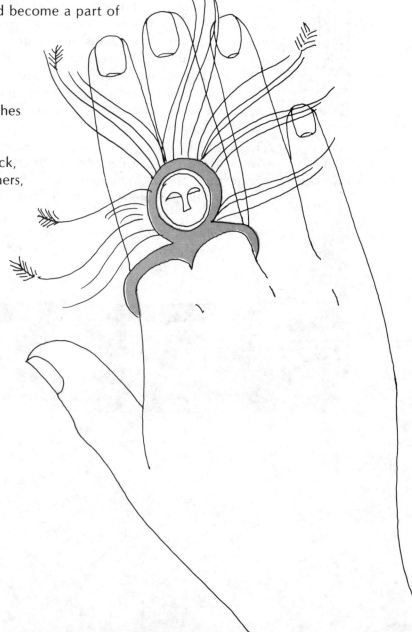

MATERIALS

Pencil
Corrugated cardboard, about 3 by 6 inches
Scissors
Poster paints and brushes
Feathers (Flexible, slender hackle, or neck, feathers are best. See Preparing Feathers, page 32.)
White glue

DIRECTIONS

1. Pencil a 2-inch circle or square onto the corrugated cardboard. Add a small rectangle about half the size of the circle or square at the bottom. Draw two finger holes on the rectangle.
2. Carefully cut out the shape of the finger mask and the finger holes. It's easiest to punch one blade of the scissors into the holes first, then to snip away the rest of each hole.
3. Trace the finger mask onto another piece of cardboard and cut it out the same way. Now you have a matching pair, one for each hand.
4. Pencil in the facial features on the front of each finger mask. They can be human or animal features, or they can be bizarre and abstract. Cut out slits for the eyes and the mouth if you like.
5. Paint the faces on the finger masks. The Eskimo most often used red, yellow, black, and white. When the front has dried, paint the backs of the masks. The backs can be painted solid or with a design, or another pair of faces can be painted so that the masks are reversible.
6. Insert feathers with a bit of glue on the shaft into the individual cells in the corrugated sides of the finger masks. A few fatter feathers can be trimmed along the shaft to about an inch from the tip to add variety.
7. Insert two fingers in the finger holes. The feathers will stick out like spokes and will wave with the motion of hands and arms when dancing.

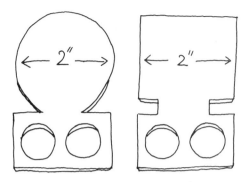

Cut shapes out of cardboard.

Paint faces or designs on the front and back of the cardboard shapes.

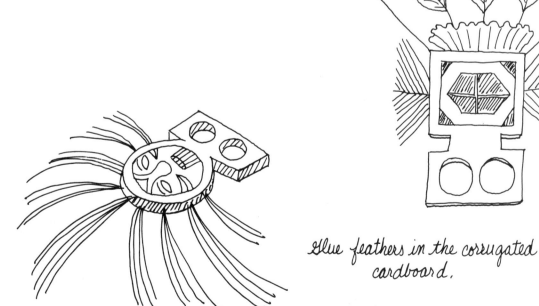

Glue feathers in the corrugated cardboard.

25

Kachina Mask

Kachinas were spiritual beings who played an important role in the Hopi religion. The Hopi believed that the kachinas encouraged the gods to provide an abundant harvest. Throughout the first half of every year, the kachina spirits left their homeland in the mountains and came down to the Hopi villages. There, they "lived" in the bodies of masked impersonators.

The impersonators were men who belonged to a special Hopi society. The men believed that when they put on a kachina mask they became the spirit that the mask represented. They made the masks themselves out of leather, adding the features of a particular kachina and painting on some of their own dream symbols. Dressed as kachinas, the men appeared at a number of ceremonial dances in the *kivas*—underground ceremonial rooms—and on the plazas of the villages.

Some of the kachina spirits were monsters whose masks and yucca whips frightened the children. Others were more good-natured and gave small gifts. Throughout the year, the children played with carved kachina dolls so that they learned to recognize the more than 200 kachina spirits that visited the Hopi.

Kachina ceremonies continue to be an important part of Hopi religion today, and it is still possible to see kachina dancers on the village plazas.

MATERIALS

3-gallon ice cream carton
Scissors
Cardboard cylinders from household paper
  rolls
Masking tape
Cardboard oatmeal container, salt container,
  or other large cardboard cylinder
Poster paints and brushes or spray paints
Glue
Fluffy feathers
Newspaper

DIRECTIONS

1. Discard the lid of the ice cream carton. If there is a metal rim along the top of the carton, pry it off carefully. (You may need to use a scissors blade.) Leave the bottom of the carton intact.

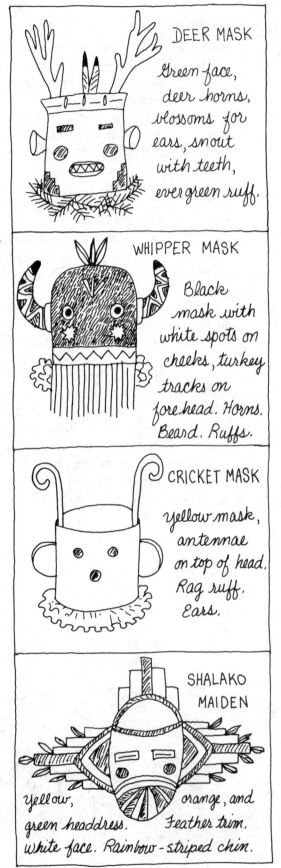

DEER MASK
Green face, deer horns, blossoms for ears, snout with teeth, evergreen ruff.

WHIPPER MASK
Black mask with white spots on cheeks, turkey tracks on forehead. Horns. Beard. Ruffs.

CRICKET MASK
Yellow mask, antennae on top of head. Rag ruff. Ears.

SHALAKO MAIDEN
Yellow, green headdress. white face. Rainbow-striped chin. orange, and feather trim.

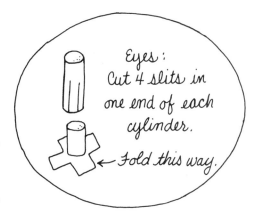

Eyes:
Cut 4 slits in one end of each cylinder.

← Fold this way.

2. Cut out sections on either side of the top of the carton for shoulder rests. Turn the carton upside down.

3. For pop-out eyes: Trim two paper roll cylinders to 3-inch lengths. Cut four slits into one end of each cylinder equidistant from one another and fold them outward. Use the uncut end to trace eyeholes on the carton where the pop-out eyes will be attached. The eyeholes should be placed high, just above where your eyes will be when you put the carton over your head. Cut out the eyeholes. Poke the unfolded end of each cylinder though an eyehole from the inside of the carton. Tape the folded ends inside the carton.

4. For a pop-out snout: Use a cardboard cylinder with a larger diameter, such as a salt or oatmeal container, and follow the directions in step 3. You may need to cut more than four slits to get the folded ends to lie down flat.

5. Cover the openings of the pop-out features with circles of plain paper cut about an inch wider than each opening all around. Hold these circles flat over the tube openings and fold and tape the excess back around the cylinders.

6. Cut a long narrow slit under the pop-out eyes. The slit should be about ¼ inch wide and should run from one eye to the other. This is where you actually see out of the mask.

7. Paint the entire mask one color. Kachina masks are traditionally green, yellow, muddy pink, white, or black. If possible, use spray paint for an even and quick-drying base coat.

8. Paint the whites and pupils of the pop-out eyes, and paint in large teeth along the front and sides of the snout. Add other painted features on the face of the mask.

9. Glue fluffy feathers along the bottom of the mask to make a furry ruff. You can add additional features as shown in the examples of various Hopi kachinas: horns made out of papier-mache; red cylinder pop-out ears; or an elaborate cardboard *tabletta*, a flat headdress.

10. Try on the mask. It will probably be a little wobbly and may be too low. Remove it and glue a thick ring of crumpled newspaper along the inside bottom of the carton (the top of the mask). Now try it on again. The kachina mask should rest on your shoulders. The crushed newspaper sits like a crown on your head to keep the mask in place. You should be able to see through the slits below the pop-out eyes.

Push the cylinder through the holes and tape inside the carton.

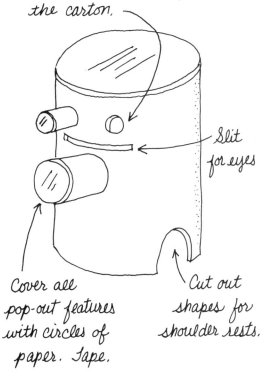

— Slit for eyes

Cover all pop-out features with circles of paper. Tape.

Cut out shapes for shoulder rests.

Paint and decorate to look like a Kachina mask.

Cornhusk Mask

Members of the Iroquois Husk Face Society wore cornhusk masks while impersonating the spirits who introduced farming to the people. These spirits with their frightening faces were called on to scare away the forces that caused illness. The masked members of this medicine society met in the longhouse of the sick person to prescribe medicines made from plants and to perform ritual songs and dances. When healthy, the cured person was encouraged to join the society to help others.

During important celebrations, the Husk Face Society and other medicine societies performed publicly. At the new year's celebration, all the medicine societies danced to assure that those cured during the year did not become sick again. Husk Face members danced carrying cornstalks and hoes and making puffing sounds through their masks. Since their masks were thought to possess the power to tell the future, Husk Face members also predicted the success of crops, the birth of children, and other events for the new year.

MATERIALS

8 ounces of cornhusks, dried or green (about
   50 husks)
1 yard of raffia
Blunt tapestry needle
Large paper plate
Scissors
2-inch section of dried corncob
Glue
Stapler
2 pieces of string, 9 inches each

DIRECTIONS

1. Tear the cornhusks into strips, about ½ to 1 inch wide. If you are using dried husks soak them in water first.
2. Tie three strips together at one end. Knot another strip to the end of each of these. Braid the strips, knotting on more as you need them.
3. When the braid is 2 feet long, tie the ends together in a knot. Make two more braids the same length. These will be for the eyes and mouth.
4. Tear other husks into 2- to 3-inch-wide strips or use them whole. Make another braid with these wider strips about 3 feet long. Trim the knotted ends on all the braids.

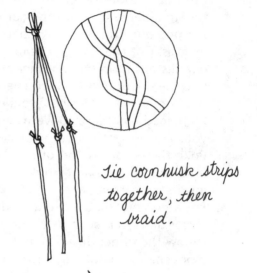

Tie cornhusk strips together, then braid.

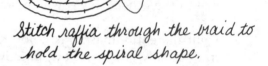

Stitch raffia through the braid to hold the spiral shape.

Sew eyes and mouth onto plate.

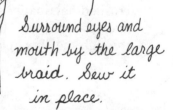

Surround eyes and mouth by the large braid. Sew it in place.

5. Thread a piece of raffia through the tapestry needle. Form a circle big enough for an eyehole with one of the short braids. Coil the rest of the braid around this eyehole, stitching the raffia through sections of the braid to hold it in a spiral shape. Make another eyehole. Now form a larger circle for the mouth and coil and stitch it.

6. To construct the face, place the eyeholes and mouth on the paper plate. Thread and knot another piece of raffia and bind the spirals in place, sewing through the plate. Circle the eyes and the mouth with the long braid and sew it in place.

7. Cut out holes in the plate behind the braided coils for the eyes and mouth.

8. For the nose, take the corncob and put glue on one side. Place it between the eyes, slightly above the mouth. Weave raffia across the cob and through the plate to hold it in place. Knot the raffia and cut it off.

9. Shred the remaining husks into strips about $\frac{1}{8}$ to $\frac{1}{4}$ inch wide. (Green husks are best to use because they curl as they dry.) Gather 10 to 12 strips and hold them so they form a fringe around the edge of the mask. Staple them in place on the plate. Fringe the entire mask this way.

10. Poke a hole halfway between the edge of the plate and the eyeholes. Insert a piece of string through both holes, pull it through, and knot it close to the mask. Hold the mask in front of your face and have someone tie the strings together so the mask fits comfortably.

Jumping Dance Headdress

Among the Hupa, Karok, and Yurok of California, there were many dances to assure peace, wealth, and an abundance of food. The Friendship Dance welcomed visitors; the Dance of Peace celebrated good relations with neighbors; and the White Deer and the Jumping Dances urged the renewal of the earth and nature each year.

Prosperous people provided costumes for the dancers as a way to demonstrate their wealth and status. Obsidian blades, flicker feathers, woodpecker scalps, dentalium shells, and white deerskins were worn as ornaments. For the Jumping Dance, dancers wore deerskin skirts, shell necklaces, and feathered headbands. The tall headdress tied to the forehead was made of fine deerskin overlaid with red woodpecker scalps and magpie, mallard, jay, and hummingbird feathers in a colorful pattern. The bright red of the woodpecker scalps and hummingbird throats was especially valuable because it was very rare.

At the beginning of the dance, a row of dancers holding ceremonial baskets bent their knees and reached toward the ground with the baskets. Then they jumped into the air and stamped down on the earth to assure its firmness for another year.

MATERIALS

Measuring cup
White glue
Small bowl
Muslin, rectangle about 12 by 9 inches
Newspaper
Poster paints and brushes
Assortment of colorful feathers (see Preparing Feathers, page 32)
Small, sharp scissors
2 pieces of cord, string, or elastic, each 10 inches long

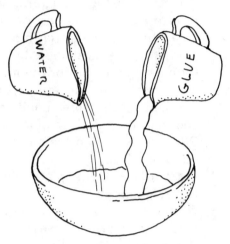

Mix water and glue.

Soak muslin.

Lay fabric on newspaper.

Hang muslin on line to dry.

30

DIRECTIONS

1. Mix ½ cup of white glue with ½ cup of water in a bowl. Soak the muslin in this mixture.
2. Spread the cloth flat on several sections of newspaper. When the cloth stops dripping, hang it up on a line or rack so that it hangs straight down. It will dry and stiffen.
3. When the cloth is dry, place it on some newspaper. Paint stripes or a geometric background for the headdress.
4. While the paint is drying, arrange the assortment of feathers by color so you can see what "paints" you have to work with. Check the backs of the feathers as well as the fronts for color. Trim the feathers into interesting shapes.
5. Glue on a variety of feathers in geometric designs. Start at the top of the headdress and work down. Leave a 1- to 2-inch margin of plain cloth on each of the 9-inch sides (as shown).
6. Let the feathers dry. Make sure they are firmly attached to the headdress.
7. Cut a tiny slit about 2 inches away from the bottom and side of each side of the headdress. Insert a piece of cord through each slit and knot the cords in the front so that they can't be pulled through.
8. Tie on the headdress and try the Jumping Dance.

1" to 2" margin of plain cloth on each side

Pull string through slit and knot.

PREPARING FEATHERS

Feathers on headdresses, staffs, and masks added colorful accents to dance costumes. Some Native American dancers also glued white, downy feathers in patterns on top of their body paint for a fluffy effect.

Before crafting with feathers, soak them overnight in warm, soapy water. Native Americans dried them in the wind, but they can be spread out to dry in some protected spot where they won't blow away. If they dry rumpled or have small kinks, hold them over the steaming spout of a teakettle for several minutes before straightening them.

Make more decorative feathers by trimming them. If some are broken or incomplete, cut those parts away and save the rest. Make interesting zigzags on the edges of some. Trim along the lower shaft of others and leave a fluff at the tip. Also cut down the center quill with a sharp knife and curl the halves the way you curl ribbons.

If some feathers are dull, brighten them by painting on colored highlights with acrylic or oil-based paints. Make longer and bouncier feathers by tying smaller feathers onto the ends of larger ones.

Native Americans also used feathers as tools to paint gourds and pots. To make a feather paintbrush, bind a feather to the end of a stick.

Overlap feathers for stripes or shapes.

Clip off the shaft and snip a zig-zag edge.

Clip off the tip and shape into a point.

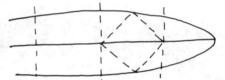

Clip off sections of a large feather and carefully trim them into diamond shapes.

Feather Fan

Native Americans greatly admired the colorful feathers of birds. Because they soared above the earth, birds were considered special messengers of the gods. Ceremonial costumes often included brilliant headdresses, headbands, capes, and fans of feathers from eagles, turkeys, hawks, woodpeckers, ducks, and hummingbirds.

Fans were for decoration and for religious ceremonies, not for cooling oneself. Some groups made fans from birch bark and feathers. Sometimes the entire wing of a small bird was made into a fan by wrapping the wing bone with cloth. The handles were usually decorated with beadwork. Feather fans were used in ceremonies because Native Americans believed they helped carry prayers swiftly to the gods.

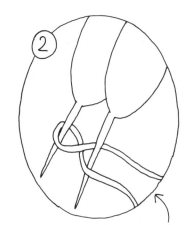

Tie the feathers together this way.

MATERIALS

4 to 7 large feathers with shafts (see Preparing Feathers, page 32)
Scissors
10-inch strand of yarn
White glue
2 leather scraps, one a 4-inch square and the other a strip, 4 by ½ inches
Small, fluffy feathers
Poster paints and brushes

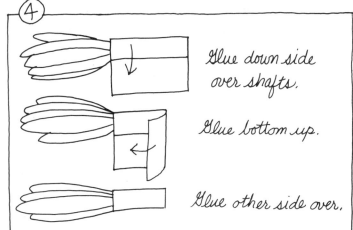

Glue down side over shafts.

Glue bottom up.

Glue other side over.

DIRECTIONS

1. Lay out the large feathers in a fan shape. Trim off any fluffy tufts near the shaft.
2. Use the yarn to bind the shafts together by doubling over the strand and putting the first shaft in the loop. Cross over the ends of the strand, put another feather next to the first, and cross the ends of the strand again. Continue crossing strands and placing feathers. When all the feathers are in place, pull the yarn tight and tie a knot.
3. Squeeze glue between the feather shafts near the yarn binding to hold them together. Let them dry.
4. Take the large piece of leather and wrap it around the shafts as shown. Glue one flap down over the shafts. Fold the bottom piece up and glue it. Now fold and glue the remaining flap over the shafts. If the leather is thick, weigh the flaps down with a book or brick until they dry.
5. Stick small, fluffy feathers into the top of the handle or glue them onto the top.
6. Paint the 4- by ½-inch leather strip with designs. When it has dried, glue it around the top of the handle.

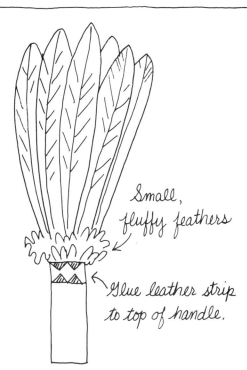

Small, fluffy feathers

Glue leather strip to top of handle.

BODY PAINT

Among the Woodlands people it was a custom to color the body with ochre, a reddish-brown mineral mixed with animal fat. That's why the first Europeans who saw Native Americans called them "redskins." Body paint was worn for all important occasions—to welcome guests, prepare for war or a hunt, dance, or play games. Although body paint had important meaning to the wearer, it had another practical purpose. The grease in the paint protected the person from wind, cold, sun, and insects.

Some designs and colors were symbolic, signifying membership in a special group or recording a brave deed. But most were very personal expressions of visions or experiences. Some patterns believed to have great power were handed down within families or could be purchased from their "owners."

To apply body paint, a person first rubbed on a coating of animal grease. A bit of dry, colored mineral powder was mixed with a little buffalo or bear fat to make the "paint." Relatives or friends helped paint designs on the back, eyes, face, and scalp where the hair parted. The Tlingit applied patterns by stamping them on with a carved wooden block. Other groups used berry juice mixed with sap instead of paint to stain the skin.

A body decoration more permanent than painting, stamping, or staining was tattooing. Among some California groups and the Eskimo, a series of small blue lines tattooed on a girl's face from the lower lip to the chin indicated she was old enough to marry. Men and women commonly wore tattoos of their clan's animal protector. The tattoos were pricked into the skin on the chest or hand with needles. Among the Eskimo, only brave hunters and women with very large and beautiful tattoos were believed to enter the afterworld when they died.

Below are some minerals that Native Americans made into body paint. To make earth paints, look for colorful soils in your environment. Clay soils are best because of their texture and fine consistency. (Pottery clay will work if you can't find soils.) Take a shovelful and let it dry out. Then pound or grind it into a fine powder with a mortar and pestle. If the soil is not very fine, mix in a little clay. When ready to paint, mix some solid vegetable shortening or petroleum jelly into a little of the soil. Rub a little on your fingers and apply it to your face, arms, or legs.

If colored soils are hard to come by, use face makeup or costume makeup sold in stores for clowns, actors, and Halloween trick-or-treaters.

Color	Minerals
Blacks	carbon soot, powdered charcoal, coal
Blue-greens	copper oxidation, malachite
Greens	pond algae (a plant, not a mineral)
Reds	hematite clay, ochre, red limestone
Whites	kaolin clay, limestone, gypsum
Yellows	limonite clay, yellow limestone

Ghost Shirt

A young Sioux named Black Elk had a vision in which the Great Spirit gave him a shirt that had magic powers to protect him from the white men's bullets. The shirt became the symbolic costume worn by men and women in a ritual called the Ghost Dance.

The Ghost Dance was part of the celebration of a new religion in the Plains region during the late 1800s. The people believed that the ghosts of their ancestors would return and reteach them their ancient ways. They believed that the white man would leave the land and that large herds of buffalo would once again roam the Great Plains.

Because buffalo and other animal skins were scarce, many Ghost Shirts were made out of unbleached muslin cloth rather than buckskin or hides. The shirts were all cut in the same pattern and sewn with the sinew of buffalo. Each individual painted different designs on his or her Ghost Shirt. The painted figures and symbols represented visions of how the world would change back to the way it had been before the white man came.

MATERIALS

Pencil
Unbleached muslin, about 1½ yards
Scissors
Needle with large eye
Waxed string, button twist thread,
   or yarn
Acrylic paints and brushes
Feathers (optional)
Beads (optional)

Paint and decorate your Ghost Shirt.

DIRECTIONS

1. Fold the piece of muslin in half. In light pencil, sketch the pattern shown onto the muslin, adjusting the measurements for fit. A good way to do this is to trace your own T-shirt and then add 4 inches all around. Add extra length in the torso and the sleeves if there's enough cloth. The shirt should fit loosely when it's finished, hanging somewhere between the hips and knees.

2. Cut out the shirt. Next, cut the neck opening along the fold, as shown. Then cut about 3 inches beyond the sides of the shirt into the sleeves to where the fringe will begin, but don't cut into the fringe yet—wait until the shirt has been sewn.

3. Thread the needle with waxed string, yarn, or thread and knot the end. Use a running stitch to sew a seam along the lengths of both sleeves. The seam should be sewn 3 or 4 inches above the bottom edge of the sleeve, starting at the point where you cut into the sleeve (step 2). Use two rows of running stitches to make an extra-strong seam.

4. Now use an over-under stitch to sew a seam along the sides of the shirt. The closer and smaller the stitches, the stronger the seams will be.

5. Now is a good time to paint the shirt, especially if you are thinking of painting the fringe. (It is difficult to paint the individual strands of fringe once they have been cut.) Use personal symbols, designs, and colors, or paint those traditionally used by Native Americans (see Native American Designs and Colors, pages 86–90.)

6. Allow the shirt to dry. Then cut the fringe in ¼-inch strips up to the seams on the sleeves. Also cut fringes along the bottom of the shirt as shown. These can be longer. Be careful not to cut into the thread that binds the shirt sleeves or the sides of the shirt.

7. Feathers and beads can be stitched in to further decorate the Ghost Shirt.

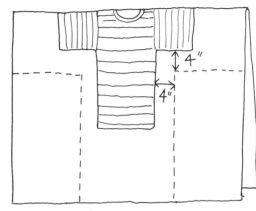

① Fold material in half. Trace your T-shirt. Add 4 inches around T-shirt. Make sleeves and torso longer by going all the way to the edges of the cloth.

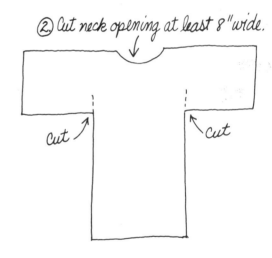

② Cut neck opening at least 8" wide.

cut   cut

③ Sew sleeves with a running stitch.

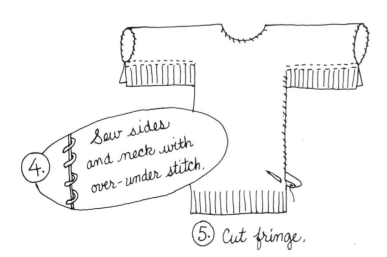

④ Sew sides and neck with over-under stitch.

⑤ Cut fringe.

Sand Painting

When a Navaho medicine singer made a "house call," he created a painting using colored soils, crushed rocks, and pollens. He painted on the bare sand floor of the sick person's house.

The singer chose a design according to whatever evil he believed was causing the sickness. First the singer and the artists and paint grinders he brought to help smoothed an area of sand. Then they took a bit of material from small pouches of yellow, white, black, red, and blue dry colors made from ground-up minerals and plants. They carefully let a trickle of color flow through their fingers onto the floor, forming a line drawing of the Holy People.

The Holy People were the gods and goddesses who lived in the sky and traveled around on rainbows, clouds, lightning bolts, and rays of sunshine. When the Holy People saw their likenesses in the sand, they drew near—near enough so that their healing powers entered the painting and absorbed the evil and illness. The sick person sat in the center of the painting while the singer chanted a healing song. Afterward, neighbors took pinches of the painting to rub on their own aches and pains. Then, for the cure to work, the sands had to be scattered before sunset. Otherwise, the evil or illness would linger in the house.

MATERIALS

Newspaper
Piece of plywood, masonite, or particle
    board
3 paintbrushes, one with fine bristles
White glue
Clean sand (Use washed beach sand or buy
    some sand from a building supply
    company.)
Sheet of paper the size of the plywood
Pencil
Large nail
Charcoal stick or chalk
"Dry paints," such as colorful soils and
    sands; small seeds; pollens; cornmeal;
    spices such as cinnamon, turmeric, pepper,
    cayenne, allspice, nutmeg, and dry
    mustard; crushed herbs; ground coffee; col-
    ored gelatin powder; sawdust
Acrylic sealer spray

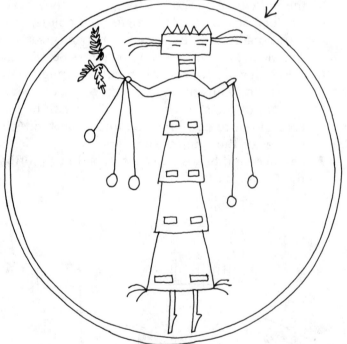

Spirit from the Mountain Chant with rattles and feather prayer offerings

DIRECTIONS

1. Cover a large work surface with newspaper. Coat one side of the piece of wood with white glue. Use a paintbrush to spread it evenly.

Coat surface with glue.

2. While the glue is still tacky, take a handful of clean sand and shake it over the board. Use a strainer if the sand is lumpy. Continue until there is a heavy, even layer of sand covering the board. Pat it gently and let it dry overnight.

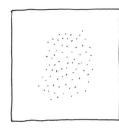

Shake sand on tacky glue surface.

3. Lift the board and shake of the excess sand. This is the background for the sand painting.

4. Sketch a design on the sheet of paper. A simple design will show up better than one with many details (see Native American Designs and Colors, pages 86–90).

5. Use a large nail to poke holes through the paper along the lines of the design. The holes should be very close together. Then hold the paper firmly on the sand-covered board and rub over the holes with a stick of charcoal or chalk. Lift the paper.

Punch holes in design. Rub charcoal through holes onto board.

6. Using the charcoal or chalk marks as guidelines, drizzle glue over an area that will be one color and spread it with the fine-tipped paintbrush.

7. Sprinkle the dry paint over the glued area. Pat the area gently and let it dry.

8. Lift the board and shake off any loose material. Then use a dry, clean paintbrush to whisk off any more loose particles. Be careful not to brush away the guidelines of the design.

Sprinkle dry paint over glued area.

9. Paint all areas of the design by following steps 6 through 8 and using one color at a time. To "erase" a mistake, put more glue on the area and sprinkle on plain sand.

10. To add details, paint them in glue on top of one color using the fine-tipped paintbrush then add a different color. Pat the area and let it dry. Then brush away any loose particles.

11. When the design is complete, spray it with acrylic sealer.

Add details over the main color.

To color sand, put some poster paint in a jar with a little water. Add a handful of sand, screw the lid on, and shake. Spread sand on newspaper to dry overnight.

Yarn Painting

Ordinary dried gourds were handy bowls for most Native Americans, but among the Huichol (in the Greater Southwest), they were also beautifully decorated and offered to the gods. The hollow inside was coated with beeswax and softened in the sun. It was then inlaid with coins, beads, mirrors, and corn kernels in a design. People took these bowls to sacred places like caves and placed them on altars. With them went prayers for plentiful crops, good health, and good fortune.

Today the Huichol make brightly colored yarn designs on plywood squares instead of beaded bowls. These yarn paintings tell Huichol stories. The pictures of animals and people in the yarn paintings are drawn to show the inside bones as well as the outsides of bodies.

MATERIALS

Dried gourd or sheet of heavy cardboard
Hacksaw or scissors
White glue
Coin (find one with an eagle or animal on it)
Pencil
Colored yarns
Colored seed beads, seeds, or dried corn
 kernels
Paintbrush

Huichol yarn painting of goddess of the earth ready for planting with rain and sun above her

DIRECTIONS

1. Cut a gourd in half with a hacksaw, or cut a large circle out of heavy cardboard with scissors.
2. Glue the coin to the center of the gourd bowl or the cardboard disk.
3. Pencil a rough sketch of a big, bold design of geometric shapes, animals, or human figures on the inside of the bowl or onto the cardboard disk (see Native American Designs and Colors, pages 86–90).
4. Cut two pieces of yarn exactly the same length. Outline part of the design with white glue. Glue the double strand of yarn to the outline of the design. Continue painting glue on the design and adding double strands of yarn until the entire design is outlined. Cut off any loose ends.
5. To make a shape or figure even bolder, outline it again.
6. To fill in the outlined areas, use different colored yarns, seeds, or beads. To fill in with yarn, always work from the outline to the middle of the design, gluing yarn along the contours. If the space inside is small, paint on glue and add a small snip of yarn. To fill in a design with beads or seeds, glue them in place.
7. With clean fingers, pat the design in place and let it dry.
8. Make a border around the edge of the bowl or disk with a double strand of yarn. Then, using a single strand of yarn, start filling in the background. Work a small area at a time, making circles inside of circles from the outside edges into the center of an area. Or make waves inside waves, or triangles inside triangles. Cut off any loose ends.

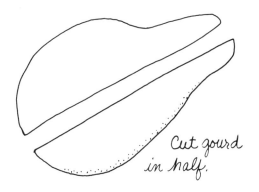

Cut gourd in half.

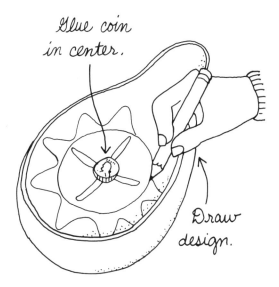

Glue coin in center.

Draw design.

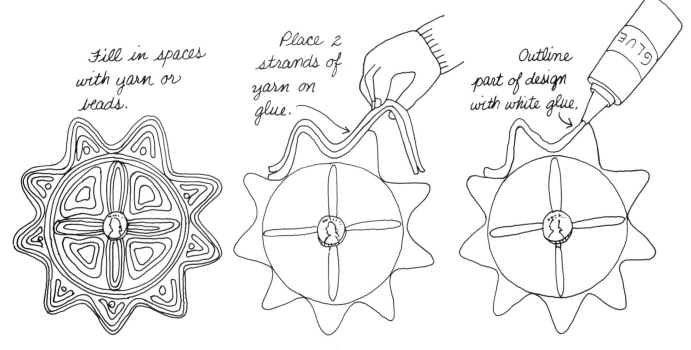

Fill in spaces with yarn or beads.

Place 2 strands of yarn on glue.

Outline part of design with white glue.

41

God's Eye

The Huichol believed that crafting an object was a way to get in touch with the spiritual world. For protection from the uncertainties of the future, the Huichol sometimes made decorative, ceremonial shields with colored yarn and sticks. These shields were called god's eyes because through them a god might keep a watchful eye over the people who made them.

To help the god see better, Huichol people wove a pupil of black yarn or a mirrored disk into the god's eye. Where the sticks crossed, they left an opening that allowed shamans (religious leaders who were believed to have powers of healing) and gods to travel easily between the spirit and earth worlds. Young Huichol children were guided on a mock pilgrimage carrying god's eyes and other offerings so that the gods might learn to recognize their faces.

The Hupa wove similar charms out of straw or yucca and hung them over babies' cradles, and among the Pueblo groups, women wore small ones as hair ornaments. Some Southwestern groups still make the offerings today and sell small god's eyes to tourists.

MATERIALS

2 straight branches, sticks, dowels, or skewers
   (The longer the sticks, the bigger the god's
   eye will be.)
Sandpaper
Balls of different colored yarn
Scissors
Small mirror or foil disk
White glue
Small feathers (optional)

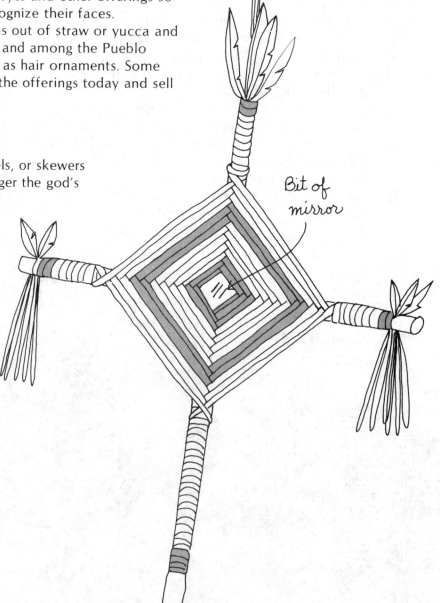

Bit of mirror

DIRECTIONS

1. Remove any twigs from the sticks. Use sandpaper to smooth any rough spots. For a diamond god's eye, use sticks of unequal length; for a square one, use sticks of equal length.

2. Cut off a piece of yarn about the length of one of the sticks. Cross the sticks and bind them together tightly with the yarn. Crisscross the yarn over the sticks several times (as shown). Tie a knot to hold them firmly in place. Snip off the loose yarn.

3. Take the ball of yarn and knot the loose end onto one of the crossbars close to the center of the sticks. Now pull the strand of yarn over the next crossbar, circle back underneath and then over the top again. Pull the strand over the third crossbar and do the same. Continue wrapping each crossbar and moving on to the next, always working in the same direction. The yarn will stretch between the crossbars and create the design.

4. To change to another color, snip the strand, leaving a 1-inch end piece. Tuck the small piece through the last wrap on the crossbar and pull tightly. Snip off the loose end. Tie on a new color and begin wrapping.

5. Continue wrapping and changing colors until the crossbars are completely covered. Or, leave the ends of the crossbars bare, tie a piece of yarn onto each, and cover each one separately with wrapped yarn. When each is wrapped, snip off the strand, tuck the end piece into the last wrap, pull tightly, and snip again.

6. Glue a small mirror or foil disk over the center of the cross.

7. Make tassels for the ends of the horizontal crossbars by wrapping yarn loosely around your fingers 5 or 6 times. Slip a small piece of yarn through the top of the loops and tie it tightly. Snip the bottom of the loops. Then tie the tassels onto the crossbars. Small feathers can be tied to the tassels with yarn, or fluffy feathers can be glued to the ends of the crossbars.

8. Tie a small yarn loop to the top of the god's eye to hang it.

Criss-cross sticks with yarn to bind them.

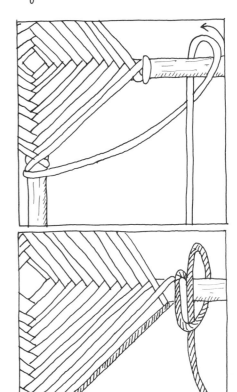

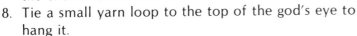

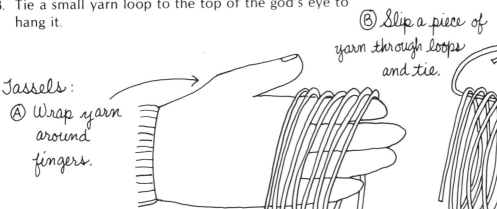

Tassels:
Ⓐ Wrap yarn around fingers.

Ⓑ Slip a piece of yarn through loops and tie.

BODY ORNAMENTS

Native Americans found many beautiful jewels in nature to wear as personal decorations. These included ivory, quills, shells, bones, feathers, seeds, claws, teeth, horns, and colorful stones. Men and women crafted them into body ornaments—necklaces, armbands, belts, earrings, and rings—for both everyday and ceremonial wear.

Some ornaments had symbolic importance, for example, a bear claw showed bravery and great strength. Others served more than one purpose. Dancers wore anklets with bells or tin cones that jingled when they moved. They also wore headdresses decorated with feathers and porcupine quills. Hair ornaments were also popular. Men and women decorated their braided hair with large shells, silver disks, beaded bands, and ribbons. Southwestern women wore feathered prayer sticks, like the god's eye on pages 42–43, in their hair.

Wearing many ornaments was a sign of wealth as well as beauty. Some ornaments had a standard value in trade and were used as money. In the West, a string of dentalium shells had great value; some men even had rulerlike tattoos on their upper arms to measure the length of a string. In the East, cylindrical beads cut from the purple section of a quahog clam shell were just as highly valued. They were called wampum. Exchanging beautifully woven belts of wampum was like signing a contract to the Iroquois. Trade always introduced new materials for crafting body ornaments. European silver coins were pounded into shiny disks and used to make belts, bracelets, and necklaces. Sometimes they were set with native turquoise stones and coral in the Greater Southwest.

Make body ornaments to wear at a Native American ceremony or around home or school. Use waxed linen thread—it's similar in feel to the animal sinew Native Americans used—and a large needle to string seeds, dried corn kernels, nuts, shells, chicken bones, or fish vertebrae. Sculpt beads or pendants out of clay. Pierce them before they have completely dried and decorate them with carved or painted designs. Dangle feathers or larger bones from a necklace, and wear many necklaces together as Native Americans did.

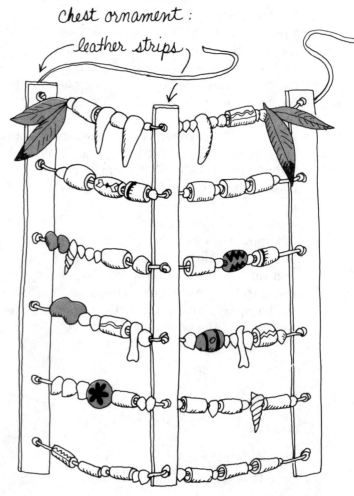

chest ornament:
leather strips

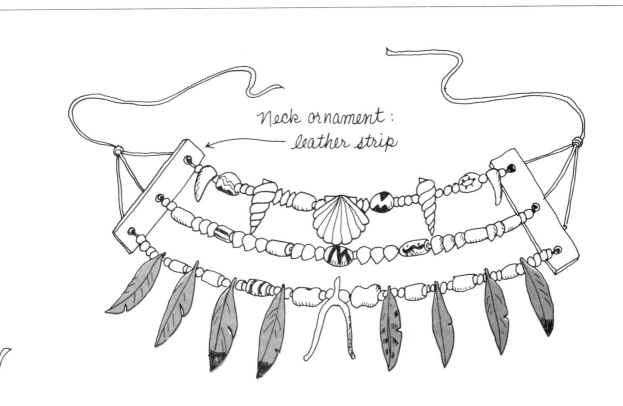

Neck ornament:
leather strip

Head ornament: leather disk with coin in center,
feathers overlapping. Tied around head
with leather strip.

Animal Effigy

By honoring many living spirits, the Zuni believed they would be blessed by good fortune while living, hunting, and farming on the earth. To the Zuni, animals and their spirits were more closely related to the gods than people were. For this reason, natural objects that resembled animals were treasured for the magical powers their spirits possessed.

At first, Native Americans simply found objects that looked somewhat like animals. Then they began to change objects slightly to make them look more like animals. Later, they carved animal shapes in stone, molded them in clay, and made pipes with animal likenesses, or *effigies,* perched on them.

From close association with animals, Native Americans knew and respected them and often wished to be like them—to have the strength of the bear or the cunning of the coyote or wolf or the hunting skill of the owl. People fashioned frog, turtle, bear, sheep, coyote, and owl and other bird effigies in hopes of gaining the traits of these animals. The Zuni owl effigy was popular with tourists in the 1800s and is still made today by Zuni craftspeople.

MATERIALS

Self-hardening clay
3 or 4 paper towels
Small pointed stick
Tweezers
Poster paints and brushes

DIRECTIONS

1. Form a ¼-inch-thick pancake of clay about 8 inches in diameter.
2. Shred and dampen three or four paper towels. Press them into a ball.
3. Wrap the clay around the paper ball, and smoothe out the creases. Form a round or oblong shape, depending on the general shape of the animal you are making.
4. Shape small pieces of clay into animal features (ears, wings, legs, beaks, snouts, tails), then press and smooth them onto the basic shape.
5. Smooth the entire surface.
6. Allow the clay to dry for a day or until it is slightly hardened. Use a stick or a paintbrush to poke a hole in the bottom of the effigy. Pull out the bits of paper inside with the tweezers.
7. When the clay has dried completely, paint the effigy.

Wrap clay pancake around ball of wet paper towels.

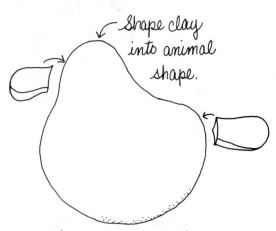

Shape clay into animal shape.

add shaped pieces of clay for ears, tail, and other features.

when dry, paint effigy.

Poke small hole in bottom and remove paper.

3

Musical Instruments

Native Americans associated music and rhythm with the world of spirits. To sing or dance or beat a drum was to offer a powerful prayer summoning the gods.

Ceremonial singing and dancing were usually accompanied by percussion-type instruments and noisemakers such as drums, rattles, rasps, and groaning sticks. Some groups also made flutes, fiddles, or musical bows to play in courting rituals. Instruments were not usually designed or played just for pleasure. Native Americans believed that spirits were called up by their instruments or actually lived inside the instruments, so they made them and played them with great respect and care.

Water Drum

Native Americans believed their ceremonial drums had magical powers; therefore, only worthy people were allowed to keep and play drums. For example, among the Plains groups, only those who had "counted coup," or earned marks of achievement in battle, were given such an honor.

Water drums were considered the most sacred of all drums among the Chippewa and their neighbors. They used water drums to accompany songs and dances in religious ceremonies. The water itself was often an important part of a ceremony. In one ceremony, after the water drum had been played, the head was removed and the drum passed around so that everyone might sip the water, which had been made holy by its use. In another, the sacred water was splashed on the spectators.

The oldest water drums were hollowed logs with a small drain hole in the side to tune them. But it became common to use an everyday vessel for the drum shell—an iron kettle, a wooden keg, or a clay pot. Water was poured into the drum to make a richer sound. Then a buckskin, decorated with symbols of the drum maker's dreams or religious visions, was dampened and stretched over the top. Properly tuned, water drums could be heard more than 10 miles away.

MATERIALS

Tapering green stick, about 15 inches long, widest part about ¼ inch in diameter
2 leather thongs or strong cords, one about 8 inches long, another long enough to go around the neck of the pot
Scissors
Piece of buckskin, chamois, or soft, thin leather (It must be large enough to stretch over the mouth of the clay pot.)
Oil or acrylic paints and brushes (Be sure to use paints that aren't soluble in water.)
Clay pot (Find one with a wide mouth and a narrower neck. Be sure it will hold water—it must be "fired" or "glazed.")

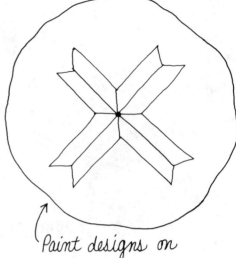

Paint designs on drumhead with waterproof paints.

Tie leather firmly over pot with thong or cord.

HOW TO MAKE THE BEATER

1. Bend the tapering end of the stick into a wide circle. Bend only about a third of the stick. If the stick is not very supple, let it soak awhile in hot water.
2. Lash the circle to the thicker part of the stick by wrapping them both with a thong or strong cord.
3. If the curved wood is smooth, knot the thong and snip off the excess. But if the wood is rough, continue wrapping all the way around the circle to make a smoother surface. Use the circular end to strike against the drumhead.

HOW TO MAKE THE DRUM

1. Decorate the buckskin or leather for the drumhead with water-fast colors before constructing the drum.
2. Soak the buckskin until it is soft and flexible.
3. Fill the clay pot no more than ¼ full with water. Not much water is needed—the Seminole used "two mouthfuls"—and too much ruins the tone.
4. Stretch the buckskin firmly and evenly over the mouth of the pot. Gather the skin around the neck so that the top remains smooth and taut. Wrap a thong or cord around the neck of the pot as tightly as possible and tie it in place. (Get somebody to help by holding the skin or wrapping the thong.)
5. It is important to keep the drumhead damp. Tip the pot or shake it so that some of the water splashes up and wets the skin.
6. Test the drum. Hit it with the beater. If the sound is hard and flat, wet the top of the drumhead again. If the sound is no more than a dull thud, allow the skin to dry and tighten a bit in the sun. Experiment until the drum is tuned so that the drum has a rich, musical sound.
7. When you're not using the drum, remove the head and store it for the next ceremonial occasion.

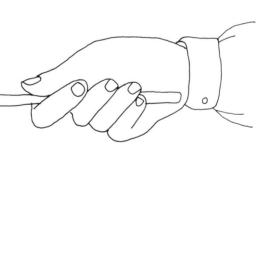

Musical Bow

The Maidu of California played a simple instrument that was much like a jew's harp. It was a short bow with a string, wire, or vine stretched across it. The player held the bow in one hand, straight out, string up, and bit down on one end of the bow or string. When the player plucked the string with a finger or a small stick, the player's mouth would act as a resonator to make the sound louder. By opening and closing the mouth, the player could vary the pitch of the single note produced by the vibrating string.

Maidu shamans (religious leaders believed to have healing powers) were said to have used the musical bow to contact spirits, and young men sometimes played it to serenade their sweethearts. But the musical bow was probably most often played just for personal enjoyment.

No other Native Americans in North America made a musical bow, but a few Central and South American groups have been known to play it. The Tucurima of Brazil called the musical bow the "instrument of solitude" because its soft sound can be heard clearly only by the person who is playing it.

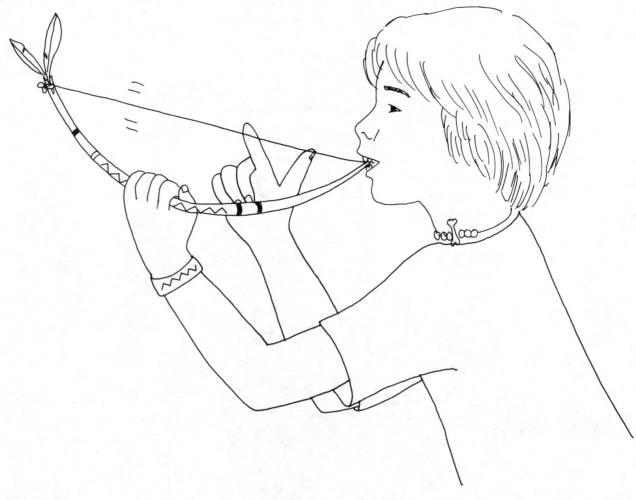

MATERIALS

Green stick, at least ³⁄₈ inch in diameter and
 about 2 feet long
Hammer and small nail or tack, or a drill
 with a ¹⁄₃₂-inch bit
Guitar string (or a string from another
 instrument)
Scissors
Poster paints and brushes (optional)
Feathers (optional)
Small, thin stick or guitar pick (optional)

DIRECTIONS

1. Strip the green stick of all leaves and small branches.
2. Carefully hammer the small nail or tack through the stick
 about ½ inch from one end. (Or carefully drill the hole
 instead, using a very small bit.) Take the nail out. Make
 another hole the same way at the other end of the stick.
 Keep the nail holes on the same side so that the line
 strung between them will be straight.
3. Knot one end of the guitar string (a nylon string is easiest
 to use). Slip the string up through one hole in the stick
 and down through the other hole as shown.
4. Pull the string more and more taut so that the stick
 becomes bowed. When the stick begins to offer
 resistance, stop.
5. Wind the excess string around the stick once or twice,
 then knot it securely. The string should still be very taut.
 Snip off the excess string.
6. The bow can be painted or feathers can be slipped into
 the knot as decoration.

HOW TO PLAY

Hold the bow in front of your mouth with the string up. Bite
down gently on the bow but keep your mouth open. Use the
other hand to pluck the string with a small stick, guitar pick,
or finger. As the string vibrates, you will hear the single note
distinctly, but others will not be able to hear it as clearly.

Open and close your mouth slowly while plucking the
string several times. The pitch of the note will change. Opening wider will bring out the higher ranges; narrowing your
mouth's opening will bring out the lower ranges.

One of the nicest things about this instrument is that it
can be played without bothering anyone.

Knot end of string.

Slip string through second hole.

Pull string very tightly to bend stick.

Wind string twice around bow and tie securely.

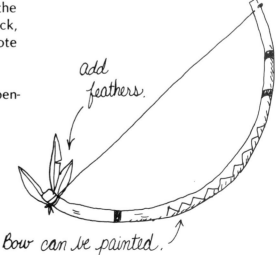

add feathers.

Bow can be painted.

51

Gourd Rattle

All kinds of rattles were shaken to the rhythm of Native American songs and dances—rattles made out of snapping turtle shells, buffalo horns, bark, carved wood, coconuts, rawhide, and gourds. Like drums, they were considered objects of great power that could be used to summon good spirits or drive away evil ones. Like feather fans and feather sticks, they were often carried by dancers as part of their costumes.

A dry gourd was a ready-made instrument whose seeds rattled when it was shaken. For some groups, the globe of the gourd represented the sun. Red feathers bound to it symbolized the sun's flames. Usually the seeds were removed and replaced with beans or pebbles, which make a louder rattle. Then a few of the original seeds were always put back in the instrument to return its powers of magic or medicine.

MATERIALS

Dry gourd (A freshly harvested gourd will dry
    in about 6 to 8 weeks, but some florists
    and crafts stores sell a variety of dry
    gourds year-round.)
Sharp knife or drill with ⅛-inch bit
Small stick or piece of wire
Stick or dowel, about ½ to 1 inch in
    diameter; length depends on the size of
    the gourd
12 pebbles or dried beans
White glue
2 leather laces or narrow leather strips (or
    pieces of strong cord) about 6 inches long
Feathers (optional)
Poster paints and brushes or colored yarn or
    strung beads
Leather strip about 1 inch wide, 12 inches
    long
Small carpet tack or utility staple
Hammer

Add pebbles or beans and a few of the original seeds.

Slide stick through bottom and top holes.

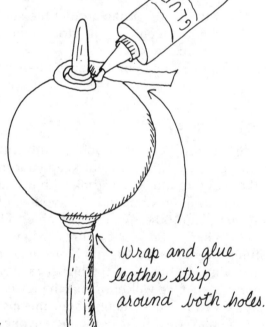

Wrap and glue leather strip around both holes.

Drive in tack or staple to attach decoration or wrist strap.

DIRECTIONS

1. Cut or drill a hole in both ends of the gourd. The holes should be just large enough so that you can slide the stick through.

2. Remove all the seeds. They will be replaced with beans or pebbles which make more noise. Scrape out any loose pulp inside the gourd with a small stick or piece of wire.

3. Slide the stick handle through the bottom hole in the gourd. Before sliding it up through the top hole, insert about a dozen pebbles or dry beans. Add a few of the original seeds to restore the rattle's powers.

4. Slide the stick on up through the hole in the top of the gourd, leaving some stick on top and enough to grip below the gourd.

5. Squeeze a good amount of white glue around the stick where it sticks out of the bottom of the gourd, and around the rim of the gourd's bottom hole. Wrap a lace or leather strip around this area once or twice. Apply more glue and continue wrapping until the cord has formed a strong plug. A few feathers can also be wrapped in as decoration.

6. Form another plug at the top of the gourd in the same way. When the glue dries, the gourd should be firmly anchored on the stick handle.

7. Paint designs on the surface of the gourd.

8. Decorate the handle by painting it or by wrapping colored yarn or a string of beads around it.

9. Hammer a staple or tack in the bottom of the handle so a wrist strap made of leather or strong cord can be attached. Give the rattle a shake.

Cherokee pattern

Pueblo pattern

SINGING AND DANCING

Native Americans had songs to celebrate almost every important life event, from naming a child to planting a field. They considered songs to be the breath of the spirits, so a person singing was a source of great powers.

Songs were sung as prayers to bring rain, abundant crops, war victories, and luck in games. There were also lullabies, love songs, work songs, and songs that told stories. Shamans sang special sacred songs as powerful medicine to heal the sick. No song was written down. It was carefully taught and passed down through each generation.

Most songs belonged to a group or clan, but some songs were personal possessions. These were "owned" and sung only by those who had inherited them or received them directly as gifts from the gods or the ghosts of ancestors. Warriors, for example, owned songs that they sang in battle to protect themselves.

Among the Arctic groups, new songs were continually composed and exchanged as gifts. The giver would often create a dance to

accompany the song and give this away as well. Sometimes a person would use a song as a weapon to challenge an enemy to a song duel. In a song, the challenger accused someone of wrongdoing. The accused person would sing back a defense and make return accusations. The people would judge whose song had been more effective, and thereby settle the dispute.

Native American ceremonies featured costumed dances along with songs. By imitating animals and birds, performers acted out the mythology of their people.

Dances varied greatly in style. Some had little movement; others were very wild. Some were performed in circles with musicians in the center; others were performed in rows with the musicians playing off to one side. Still others were performed by only one dancer. It was very important that no performer make a mistake for fear of offending the gods who were being honored. In medicine ceremonies, a mistake in a song or dance meant beginning the ritual all over again.

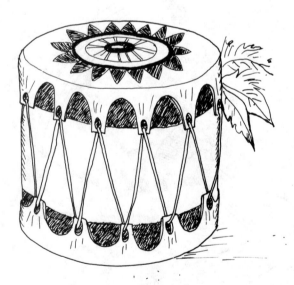

Kiowa eagle dance

Buzzing Toy

Native American children played with a simple noisemaker that hummed and buzzed on a piece of twisted string. They strung a small piece of bone, ivory, wood, dried gourd shell, or clay disk on a sinew cord. The cord was made into a loop and twisted to "wind up" the toy. Children pulled the string tight and then let it loosen to make the disk spin. The spinning disk and vibrating string made a humming or buzzing sound. This toy did not have any ceremonial use or meaning—it was just for fun.

Tie ends.

Painted clay disk, 2" in diameter

MATERIALS

Self-hardening clay or large coat button
Cookie cutter or jar or glass
Small stick or pencil
Poster paints and brushes
2 small pegs or bones (Split a wishbone in two.)
About 20 inches of leather thong or waxed string or cord

Small bones or pegs

DIRECTIONS

1. Make a ¼-inch-thick pancake with the clay. Use the cookie cutter (or the rim of a jar or glass) to cut out a small disk, about 2 inches in diameter. (A large coat button can also be used. If the button is used, skip to step 3.)
2. Poke two holes in the center of the disk with a small stick or a pencil point. Use the same tool to scrape a design on the clay. Allow the clay to dry for a day or two.
3. Paint the disk (or button). Also paint the pegs or bones.
4. Thread the thong or cord through both holes in the disk (or button). Tie the ends of the thong together.
5. Knot the end loops of the cord around each of the pegs or bones to make handles.
6. Wind the handles in opposite directions until the cord is twisted.
7. To make the toy hum and buzz, pull the cords tight and then let them loosen. The disk in the middle will spin and bob up and down and sing.

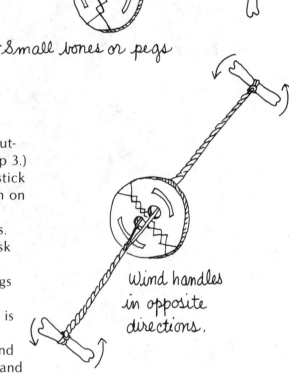

Wind handles in opposite directions.

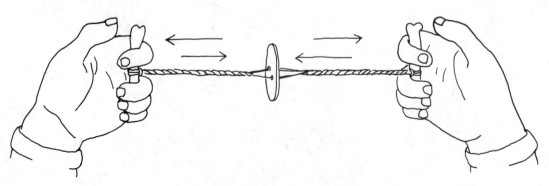

Groaning Stick

Navaho Lightning Dancers whirled a thin piece of wood on a whip above their heads to make the sound of great winds and distant thunder. This noisemaker was called a "groaning stick." It sang with the voice of the thunderbird, who, according to Navaho mythology, flapped its wings to make thunder and blinked its eyes to make lightning.

Sometimes the wood for the groaning stick came from trees that had actually been struck by lightning. The wood was decorated with symbols of the thunderbird, lightning, rain, and clouds. In most areas, the groaning stick summoned rainstorms, but on the wet Northwest Coast, it appealed for fair weather.

Some Native American children adopted the noisemaker as a toy. But because of the stick's special power, Hopi children were not allowed to play with it except in spring when the wind it called forth could do no damage.

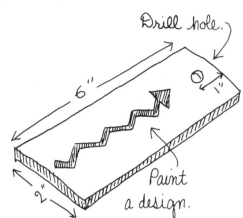

Drill hole. 6" 1" 2" Paint a design.

MATERIALS

Wooden fruit or vegetable crate or wood shingle
Hammer
Small saw
Drill with 1/8-inch bit or large nail
3 feet of heavy twine
Scissors
Poster paints and brushes

Measure string from arm's length to opposite shoulder.

DIRECTIONS

1. Pry off one of the slats from the side of a wooden crate with a hammer. Saw the slat to make a piece of wood about 2 inches wide and 6 inches long.
2. Drill a hole in the center of the wood about 1 inch from the top (one of the 2-inch sides). Or hammer a large nail in *gently*—be careful not to split the wood. When the hole is made, remove the nail.
3. Thread one end of the heavy twine through the hole. Tie the twine to the wood with several very tight knots.
4. Hold the piece of wood at the point where the string is attached. With that arm outstretched, pull the twine across to the opposite shoulder with the other hand. This is a good length, so cut the string here.

Swing overhead with arm outstretched.

5. Paint the groaning stick with symbols of the thunderbird, lightning, rain, or clouds.
6. To use the groaning stick: Wrap some of the twine around one hand. Lift that arm over your head and swing the groaning stick around. After a few turns, it should begin to hum and buzz. If it doesn't, try adjusting the length of the string by wrapping more or less around the hand. Be careful when stopping—lower your arm slowly, keeping it outstretched in front of you. The groaning stick will stop spinning and fall to the ground.

Note: A groaning stick can be dangerous if it is not used properly. Always use it outside and a good distance away from people or other obstacles. And stay out of the way of someone else who is playing with one!

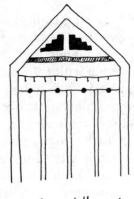

Clouds with rain

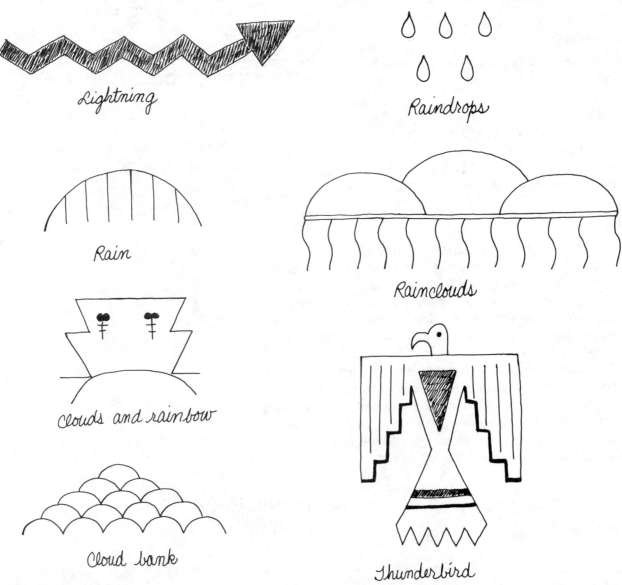

Lightning

Raindrops

Rain

Rainclouds

Clouds and rainbow

Cloud bank

Thunderbird

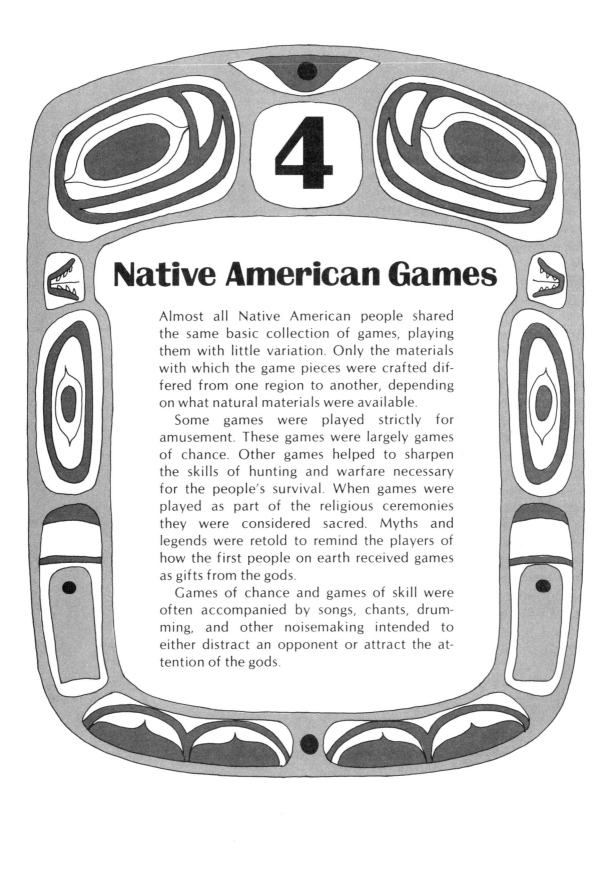

Native American Games

Almost all Native American people shared the same basic collection of games, playing them with little variation. Only the materials with which the game pieces were crafted differed from one region to another, depending on what natural materials were available.

Some games were played strictly for amusement. These games were largely games of chance. Other games helped to sharpen the skills of hunting and warfare necessary for the people's survival. When games were played as part of the religious ceremonies they were considered sacred. Myths and legends were retold to remind the players of how the first people on earth received games as gifts from the gods.

Games of chance and games of skill were often accompanied by songs, chants, drumming, and other noisemaking intended to either distract an opponent or attract the attention of the gods.

Kick-Stick Race

A Zuni kick-stick race was like a long-distance soccer game. The Bow Priests called for these footraces during the planting season—the spring and early summer—as prayers for rain. The Zuni believed that chasing a rolling stick southward along the riverbed would start the streams racing down the canyons and gulleys of their dry land.

Four days before a race, the Bow Priest would announce the event. Each society would enter several runners on its team. Two teams would race at a time, one representing the older Twin War God, the other representing the younger Twin. Each team made a *tikwawe,* or kicking stick, as long as a person's middle finger, with one of the Twins' special markings on it.

Before the race, there was much ritual and preparation. Early in the morning, the runners exercised. They washed their hair and braided in an arrow point, a symbol of swiftness. They painted the symbols of their societies on their chests. The Bow Priest blessed them with feathered prayer sticks.

Everybody gathered to watch the race. The Bow Priest sprinkled sacred cornmeal over the starting line four times. The fourth time was the signal to start. At the signal, the team leaders tossed their sticks in the air ahead of them with their toes, and their teammates chased after the sticks, kicking them farther along the course. The course was 4 to 25 miles long and full of natural obstacles such as sand, rocks, hills, brush, and holes. Only the feet or toes could be used to move the stick forward.

The Zuni thought the stick rolling ahead of them made them run faster. So, when they wanted to hurry home from the corn fields, they would break off a piece of branch and kick it in front of them to speed their return.

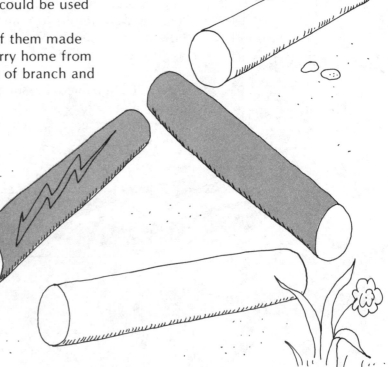

MATERIALS

Broomsticks, long dowels, or long branches
  (all 1 inch in diameter)
Small saw
Red poster paint and brush
Body paints (see Body Paint, page 34) or
  plain T-shirts and acrylic or other color-fast
  paints and brushes
String (long enough to mark a starting line) or
  powder
Cornmeal

DIRECTIONS

1. When a race has been announced and runners chosen for
   two teams, each team makes a *tikwawe,* or kicking stick,
   by sawing a 4-inch length from a broomstick (or dowel or
   branch).
2. The team that represents the older Twin War God paints
   a red stripe around the middle of the kicking stick and
   red stripes around each end. The team that represents the
   younger Twin paints only one red stripe around the middle. Other team designs and symbols may also be painted
   on the kicking sticks.
3. Each team designs a group symbol to indicate speed or
   strength, such as an arrow, a hummingbird, wings, a
   comet, a thunderbolt, a bullet, or a roadrunner. Wear the
   symbols as body paint or paint them on T-shirts.

HOW TO PLAY *(Two teams with 3–6 runners each)*

When the spring weather arrives, announce plans for a kick-
stick race. Give racers at least 4 days notice to train and prepare. Assign 3 to 6 runners to a team.

   The day of the race, set up a long course—for example,
the length of a soccer or football field. Mark the starting line
with a length of string or powder. Have each team choose a
leader to kick off. Ask someone who is not running to start
the race.

   The starter sprinkles cornmeal over the starting line four
times, wishing the runners strength and speed. The fourth
time is the signal. The leaders lift their kick-sticks on their
toes, tossing the sticks up and ahead of them. The other
team members race after the sticks, kicking them up to
teammates who are running ahead. If a runner misses,
another teammate comes up behind and takes over the pass.
The first team to kick its stick the length of the course and
back again wins.

Paint symbol on T-shirt.

Plum-Stone Basket Gamble

Dice games were played for stakes as small as a few shell beads or as large as all of a person's wealth. For their dice, the Eskimo carved seal bones and the ivory tusks of walrus. Pueblo groups decorated split cane. Other Native Americans used sticks, beaver teeth, corn kernels, shells, pottery disks, or buffalo bones. Another very common material for making dice was peach or plum stones.

Sometimes dice games also had ceremonial importance. The Zuni believed that the Twin War Gods, who loved playing games of all kinds, were very fond of dice games. Zuni stick dice, made out of the same materials as their weapons, were decorated with symbols of war, and were left as offerings on the War Gods' altar. The flat basket that the Hopi used to toss the dice represented a warrior's shield. The Onondaga gambled, men against women, at the new year White Dog festival to predict the success of the next harvest. If the men won, the ears of corn would be large like the men; if the women won, the ears would be smaller like the women.

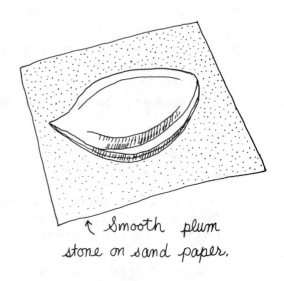

↖ Smooth plum stone on sand paper.

MATERIALS

4 plum, peach, or apricot stones (pits)
Sandpaper
Black poster paint and brushes
Acrylic sealer spray
50 sticks, pebbles, or beans for counters
Blanket (to sit on while playing)
Shallow basket or wooden bowl (to hold
   dice)

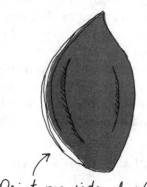

Paint one side of plum stone black.

Paint a symbol on other side.

DIRECTIONS

1. Allow the plum stones to dry at least overnight after removing them from the fruit and cleaning them thoroughly.
2. Sand the rough areas of the pits smooth. The easiest way to do this is to lay a sheet of sandpaper flat on a table, hold the sandpaper down, and rub the pit on the coarse surface.
3. Paint one side of each stone black. Paint a small symbol or decoration on the other side. The black side is the face-down side. The decorated side is the face-up side.
4. When the paint has dried, spray the dice with an acrylic sealer so the paint won't scratch or chip.
5. The counters can be decorated with stripes of paint.

HOW TO PLAY *(2 players)*

Two players sit facing each other on a blanket. The dice are placed in the basket or wooden bowl. The counters are placed in a pile between the players. The first player shakes the dice in the basket and then whacks the basket down on the blanket sharply to make the dice jump and turn. These are the scoring combinations:

1 face-up, 3 face-down: 1 point
1 face-down, 3 face-up: 1 point
2 face-up, 2 face-down: 0 points
4 face-up: 5 points
4 face-down: 5 points

If the player scores, he or she takes the same number of counters from the pile and tosses again. When a nonscoring combination comes up, the basket is passed to the other player. After all 50 counters have been won from the middle pile, players take counters from one another until one player has won all the counters.

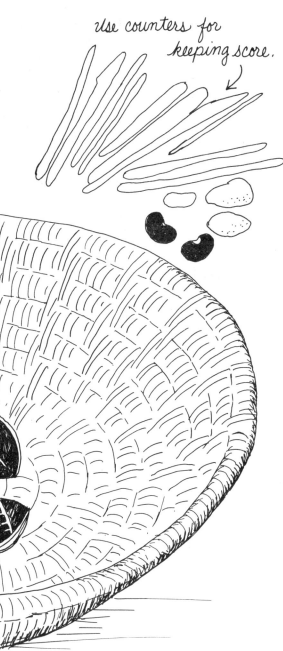

use counters for keeping score.

Hidden-Ball Game

Guessing games, such as the hidden-ball game, were very popular with Native Americans. According to Apache mythology, the hidden-ball game was played at the beginning of the world—birds and other daytime creatures against owls and nighttime hunting animals—to settle a dispute about whether or not there should be daylight.

The hidden "ball" was really any small object—a piece of bone, wood, or horn; a plum stone; a corn kernel; a bean; a pebble; or a bullet. The containers for hiding the ball also varied from group to group. The Pima and Papago hid the ball in one of four cane tubes; the Hopi and Zuni hid it in cottonwood cups; the Chippewa and Sioux, in moccasins.

The object of the game was simple. One side had to guess in what place the other side had hidden the ball. The hiding team would sing a special song while the leader of the team hid the ball, performing sleight-of-hand tricks to confuse the guessers.

The hidden-ball game was usually played only at special times. The Zuni played in the early spring to determine whether the planting season would be wet or dry. Their two teams represented the water gods and the wind gods. The Apache played only on winter nights. They believed that if the hidden-ball song was sung at any other time, the singer would be bitten by a rattlesnake.

MATERIALS

Bamboo stalk with at least 4 joints, about 1
   inch in diameter
Small saw or hacksaw
Poster paints and brushes
Round, flat stone no bigger than a silver
   dollar
Sand, about a shoebox-full
100 beans, toothpicks, beads, or other small
   objects for counters
2 small sticks
Small object such as a marble or a bean

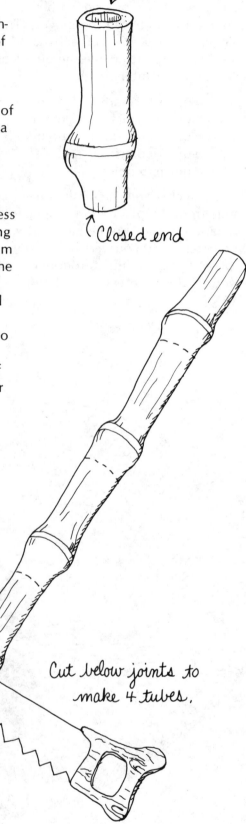

Open end

Closed end

Cut below joints to make 4 tubes.

DIRECTIONS

1. Cut the bamboo below the joints as shown to make 4 tubes.
2. Decorate each tube differently. Some groups decorated the tubes with symbols and colors for the four compass directions: north, south, east, west (see Native American Designs and Colors, pages 86–90).
3. Paint one side of the stone black.

HOW TO PLAY *(Two players)*

Two players (or two teams) sit opposite each other. The sand is dumped in a pile in the middle; so are the counters. Each player has a pointing stick. The four empty cane tubes are set open ends up into the sand, very close to each other.

The players first flip the stone disk to see who goes first. The first player holds the bean or marble—the ball—loosely in one hand and passes that hand over the tubes several times. During one of the passes, the player drops the ball into one of the tubes. The same player drops some sand into all of the tubes so that it is impossible to tell by looking inside which tube contains the ball.

The second player makes a guess by pointing at a tube with the pointing stick. That tube is emptied to see if it holds the ball. If not, the player guesses again. Depending on how many guesses it takes, the second player picks up a certain number of counters. Then the second player hides the ball, and the first player guesses. After all the counters have been won, the players take from each other's pile until one player wins all the counters.

Here's how to score:

First guess correct: 10 points
Second guess correct: 6 points
Third guess correct: 4 points
Last guess correct: 0 points

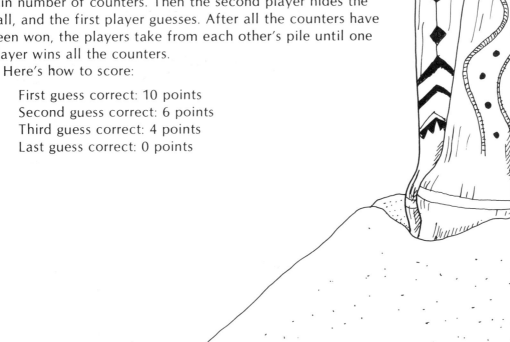

65

Corncob Darts

A very common Native American game was throwing an arrow or spear at a rolling hoop target. This hoop and pole game developed skills for successful hunting and warfare. In the Southwest, the playing materials were feather-tipped corncob darts and cornhusk rings or yucca ball targets.

The Zuni played corncob darts at the beginning of winter as an offering to the Twin War Gods, who taught the Zuni the art of warfare. The two feathered darts represent the Twins, the children of the Sun. At other times the Zuni played for rainfall. On a field sprinkled with sacred cornmeal, the first player to strike the yucca ball gave thanks for the coming rain.

In a Hopi ceremony, two women shot at a bundle of cornhusks, imitating lightning striking a cornfield. This assured fertile fields and an abundant harvest.

MATERIALS

2 dried corncobs (Scrape the cobs clean and
 let them dry in the sun for a few days.)
2 straight sticks, about ¼ inch in diameter
 and 6 inches long, each with one pointed
 end (Sharpen one end in a pencil
 sharpener.)
4 feathers with shafts, at least 3 inches long
 (Flexible, rather than stiff, feathers are
 best.)
White glue
Knife
2 pieces of yarn, 3 or 4 inches each
Ball of raffia

For Cornhusk Ring (optional):
½-inch-thick rope, 12 inches long; or round
 hoop, 6 inches in diameter
Small piece of string
15 to 30 cornhusks, dried or green

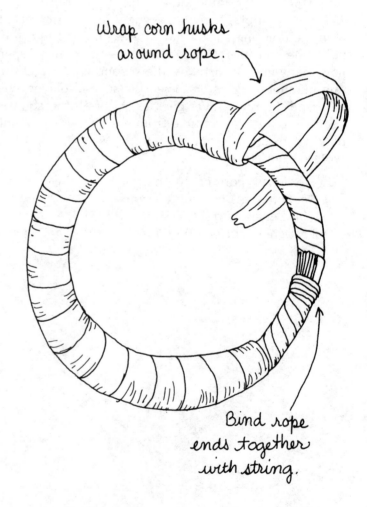

Wrap corn husks around rope.

Bind rope ends together with string.

HOW TO MAKE A CORNCOB DART

1. Cut or break off a 3-inch section of corncob.
2. Carefully insert the pointed end of the stick into the soft center of the cob. Slowly push it through. Be sure that the stick stays in the center of the cob, or the dart will be unbalanced.
3. Extend the pointed end of the stick about 2 inches past the end of the cob. There should be 1 inch of stick at the other end.
4. Push the shafts of two feathers into the top of the cob next to the stick.
5. Put glue on a piece of yarn, wrap it around the bottom of the feathers, and bind them to the stick. Cut off the extra yarn.
6. Make another dart the same way.

HOW TO MAKE A CORNHUSK RING (optional)

1. Form a circle with the rope, overlapping the ends. Use string to bind the rope ends on top of one another.
2. Wrap a cornhusk around the rope. (Soak the husks in water first if they are dried.) Overlap the previous wrap each time you wrap the husk around.
3. About 2 inches before the end of the husk, start wrapping with a new husk. Wrap over the endpieces to hide and bind them.
4. When the entire ring is wrapped, tie the last wrap with a small strip of husk.

HOW TO PLAY (2 players)

Place the target—either a ball of loose raffia or the cornhusk ring—in a pit of sand, soft dirt, or grass. Mark a line 10 feet away. The player stands behind the line and tosses a corncob dart at the target. Then the other player tosses. If the dart sticks in the raffia ball or lands within the cornhusk ring, the player scores 1 point. However, if the other player also hits, neither one scores. Play to 25 points.

For a much more difficult game, one player rolls the ring across a smooth field in front of the other player. The player aims and shoots for the moving target and tries to make it fall *on* the dart, scoring a point. Players alternate rolling and shooting until one reaches 10 points.

Carefully insert pointed end of stick into cob.

2"

Insert 2 feathers close to stick.

Yucca ball target →

Jackrabbits Hit

The Zuni played a game similar to badminton called Jackrabbits Hit. The shuttlecock, or "birdie," was a woven packet of green cornhusks with two or four feathers bound in at the top. The paddle was simply the palm of one hand. The game was called jackrabbits hit because the sound of the hand hitting the shuttlecock sounded like jackrabbits hopping over crusted snow.

Other Native Americans played versions of Jackrabbits Hit, calling it by other names and making the game equipment out of other materials. The Pima, for example, made shuttlecocks out of pieces of corncob stuck with feathers. In the Northwest, the Makah made paddles out of cedar wood and batted shuttlecocks made from plugs of wood and feathers.

MATERIALS

Green cornhusks
2 or 4 feathers at least 3 inches long (The
   flexible kind are best.)
Raffia or yarn, 1 yard
Scissors
White glue

DIRECTIONS

1. Form a cross with two wide, green cornhusks. Fold another husk into a flat square and place it in the center of the cross.
2. Lift up the two ends of the bottom husk, allowing them to curl inward a bit. Hold them in a pinch together at the center, over the rolled-up husk.
3. Lift up the ends of the other husk and gather them to the ends of the first pinched husk. Now pinch all four ends together. The rolled-up husk should have disappeared inside this wrapping.
4. Let up on the pinch just enough to insert the feathers into the center of the bundle.
5. Wrap raffia around the base of the pinched ends and continue winding upward until the husk ends are bound securely around the shafts of the feathers. Stop about ½ inch from the husk ends. Knot the raffia by tucking it under itself once or twice, then snip it. Glue the snipped end around the bound husks to make it tidy.

① Form a cross with 2 cornhusks.

Roll up another cornhusk and place in center of cross.

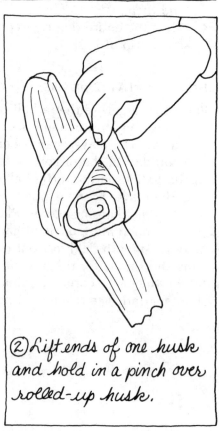

② Lift ends of one husk and hold in a pinch over rolled-up husk.

6. Trim the ends of the husks so that they stick out evenly above the raffia binding.
7. Fluff the feathers and pull them gently so that they are well balanced in the center of the shuttlecock.

HOW TO PLAY *(2 or more players)*

Two or more players take turns trying to bat the shuttlecock in the air with the palm of one hand. The first one to hit it 10 times without missing wins the round. As the players get better, the winning number of hits can be increased up to as high as 100 hits.

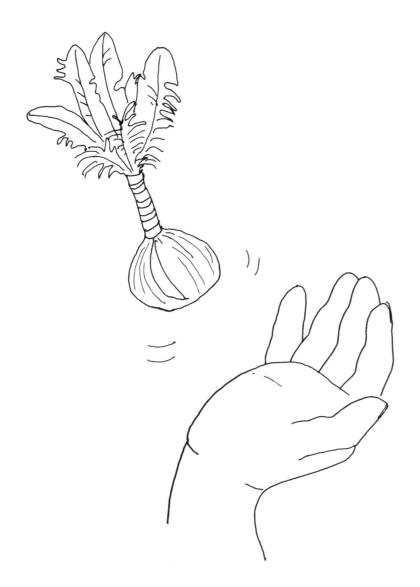

③ *Gather 2 other ends and pinch all 4 ends together.*

④ *Insert feathers in center of bundle.*

⑤ *Wrap raffia securely around pinched ends and feather shafts.*

Harpoon the Seal

This game imitates harpooning a seal through its breathing hole in the ice. During winter when the waterways were iced over, the Eskimo used special methods to hunt the animals that swam beneath the ice layer. With the help of huskies, a hunter would search for the snow-covered breathing holes that seals scratched in the ice. A line was dropped through a breathing hole into the water, then a feather bob was attached to the line above the ice. The hunter waited. When a seal swam close by, the line moved and the feather shook. Harpoon poised, the hunter would strike when the seal came up for air.

Before butchering the seal, the Eskimo tried to please its spirit by giving it a drink of fresh water, mittens, and new snow to lie on. They hoped that news of the good treatment would reach other seals and encourage them to be easy prey.

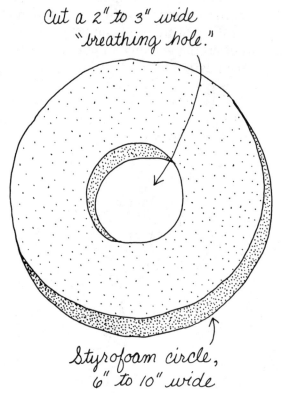

Cut a 2" to 3" wide "breathing hole."

Styrofoam circle, 6" to 10" wide

MATERIALS

Styrofoam circle, about 6 to 10 inches in
 diameter
Knife
Leather thong or string, about 20 inches long
Tapered stick, about 12 inches long
Corrugated cardboard, 4 by 10 inches
Pencil
Scissors
Seal pattern (See illustration.)
Black felt-tip pen

DIRECTIONS

1. Cut a 2- to 3-inch circle out of the center of the styrofoam to make a breathing hole in the "ice."
2. Tie the leather thong to the blunt end of the stick. This is the harpoon. (Note: The other end should taper, but should not come to a sharp point.)
3. Trace the pattern for the seal onto cardboard and cut it out.
4. Cut out the harpoon hole in the seal's body. Add eyes, a nose, whiskers, and flippers to the seal with a black felt-tip pen or other marker.

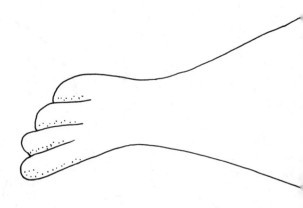

HOW TO PLAY *(2 players)*

One player is the seal and holds the ice patch with the breathing hole steady in one hand. With the other hand, the player makes the seal swim under the ice and occasionally surface to breathe at the hole. The other player is the hunter and holds the harpoon in one hand and the line in the other.

The hunter waits for the seal to appear and then drops the harpoon through the breathing hole and tries to hit the hole in the seal to spear it. When the seal is hit anywhere, it becomes paralyzed with fear and stops swimming. It is then an easy target for a quick hunter who may strike one more time while the seal is motionless. If the harpoon misses the seal, the hunter uses the line to retrieve it and must wait for the seal to appear again.

When the seal is harpooned, the players exchange roles.

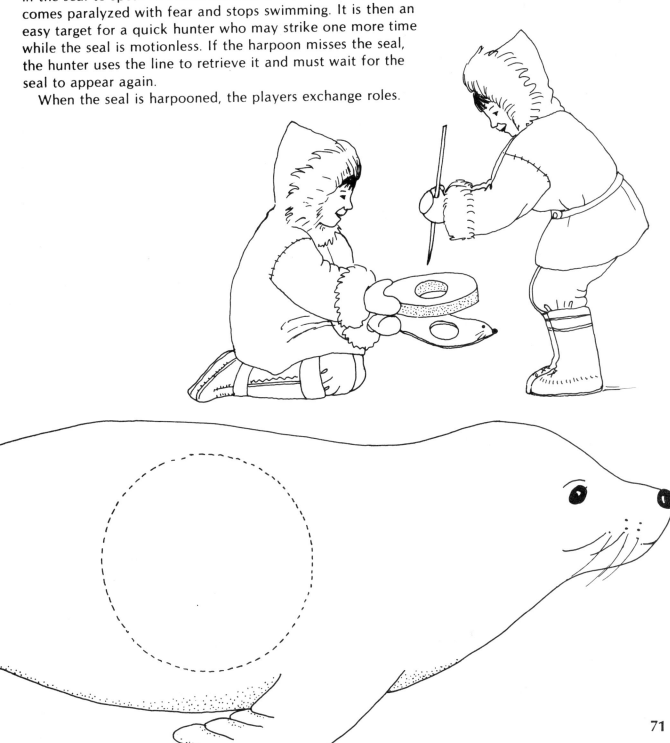

CHOOSING TEAMS

The Inuit, or Eskimo (as the French fur traders called them), choose teams for their games according to when the players were born.

Those born in the summer months are the "sea pigeons," birds seen during the summer by the Inuit fishermen when they paddle their kayaks over water. Those born in the winter months are the "ptarmigans," birds hunted on the coast whose plumage changes color with the seasons, turning snow-white in the winter.

Those players born in "freeze" (autumn) or "break-up" (spring) can choose or be chosen by either side. But the "sea pigeons" and "ptarmigans" themselves never play on the same team.

Ring and Pin Toss

Ring and pin toss was known as a lovers' game and used in courtship among the Penobscot of the Woodlands and the Cheyenne of the Plains. A boy would ask a girl to play. He would toss the rings and spear them with the pin until he missed and his turn ended. Then the girl would take her turn. If she liked the boy, she would play until the end of the game. But if she didn't like him, she would hand the game back to him the first time she caught a toss and refuse to continue playing.

Many materials were made into rings, including deer bones (Sioux), fish vertebrae (Hupa), dried gourd (Pima), and acorn caps (Mission). The pin was a pointed bone, stick, or needle. The rings were suspended on a long thong tied on one end to the pin and on the other to a piece of rawhide to prevent the rings from slipping off. In the Cree version of the game, the last ring of bone (nearest the rawhide) was painted blue-green and called the "last-born child." Catching this one meant the player instantly won the game.

MATERIALS

Leather thong, about 15 inches long
Tapered (but not sharp) stick, about 15
    inches long
3 to 6 bones with holes in the centers about
    ½ inch wide (see Bleaching Bones, page
    17), or curtain rings, large washers, or
    limpet shells
Sandpaper
Rawhide or stiff leather scrap, wider than the
    bones (or other rings)
Large hole punch
Blue-green poster paint and brush

DIRECTIONS

1. Tie the thong to the middle of the stick.
2. Use sandpaper to smooth any rough spots on the bones.
3. Slip the bones onto the thong.
4. Punch one large hole in the center of the rawhide and some random smaller holes (but large enough for the stick to enter). At one end, punch a hole ½ inch from the edge in which to insert the thong.
5. Knot the thong securely onto the rawhide.
6. Paint the bone closest to the rawhide blue-green.

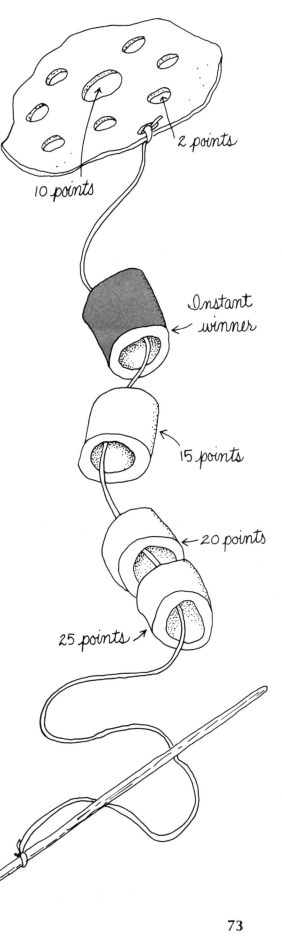

2 points

10 points

Instant winner

15 points

20 points

25 points

HOW TO PLAY (2 or more players)

Hold the stick firmly in one hand. Swing that arm up and forward to toss the rings. As the rings fall, try to spear one or more of them with the point of the stick, or try to spear a hole in the rawhide.

Here's how to score: The small holes in the rawhide count 2 points. The large hole counts 10 points. The bone in front of the blue-green ring counts 15 points, and each bone closer to the stick goes up in value by 5 points. The blue-green bone, if caught, is an instant win. A player continues to toss until he or she misses the rings and leather target altogether. Then the next player takes a turn. At first the game may seem difficult, but after a few rounds, you'll be ready for a game played to 100 points.

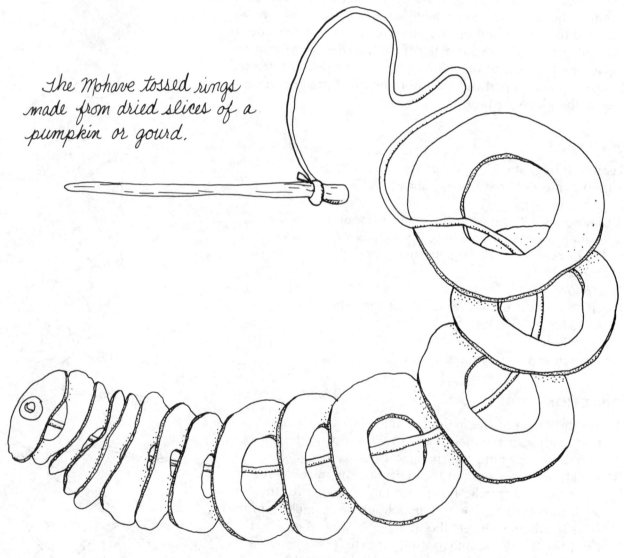

The Mohave tossed rings made from dried slices of a pumpkin or gourd.

Native American Cooking

Native Americans ate many foods unknown to the first European settlers, such as corn, potatoes, pumpkins, squash, string beans, peppers, sunflower seeds, peanuts, maple syrup, tomatoes, strawberries, and wild rice.

Besides plant foods, Native Americans ate game animals, wild fowl, and fish. Each group ate whatever the environment had to offer. The California and Intermountain peoples gathered plant foods. People on the Plains hunted most of what they ate. Groups in the Southeast and Southwest mostly farmed, and others in the Northwest and Arctic areas fished and hunted at sea.

Hospitality was very important to all Native Americans. Guests were offered a meal even if a family was poor or short of food. A Zuni visitor, for example, was invited to sit and eat even before the reason for the visit was given. Out of the same politeness, a guest would accept the invitation, eat all that was offered, and show appreciation by smacking the lips and burping.

Dried Fruit

During the harvest season, Native Americans prepared for the winter months ahead by drying foods. Dried foods kept longer without spoiling and were easier to store and carry. When out fishing or hunting or gathering, people enjoyed a small meal of dried fruit, nuts, and, perhaps, pemmican (see page 77).

After the harvest, the Pueblo peoples filled basket trays with fruits and corn and put them on rooftops to dry. They cleaned flat rocks and used them as community drying racks for berries and cherries. They cut strips of watermelon, squash, pumpkin, and cantaloupe and hung them up to dry. The melon and squash pieces were especially good for winter stews, often sweetened with a few dried peaches.

MATERIALS

Fresh fruit such as blueberries, blackberries,
   raspberries, apples, peaches, cherries,
   apricots, or pears
Knife
Lemon juice
Flat board or tray (nonmetallic)
Cheesecloth, 2 pieces, each large enough to
   cover the board or tray

DIRECTIONS

1. Wash the fruit thoroughly. Get rid of any leaves, stems, or pits.
2. If the fruit is large, cut it into ½-inch slices. Squeeze lemon juice on the slices to keep them from turning brown.
3. Cover the board or tray with cheesecloth. Place the slices or whole fruits on it. They should not touch one another.
4. Cover the fruit with a second layer of cheesecloth. Move the board or tray into a sunny spot. Let the fruit dry outside for several days. Turn the fruit three or four times. Take the tray in each night and in the daytime if it rains. Depending on the kind of fruit, it may take from 2 to 6 days to dry.
5. Store the fruit in a covered jar or in a refrigerator.

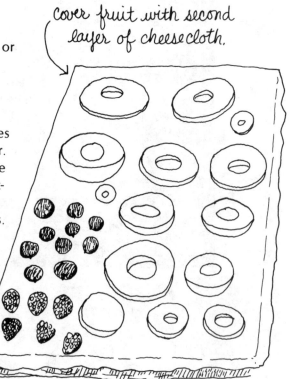

cover fruit with second layer of cheesecloth.

Cover board with cheesecloth.

Flat wooden board or tray

Pemmican

Pemmican was the most important food staple of groups in the Plains area. It was a mixture of pounded dried meat, berries or dried fruits, and buffalo fat, which held the mixture together. Pemmican was lightweight, full of protein, and kept for a long time without spoiling—three important features to the hunters who traveled for long periods at a time in search of buffalo. The Plains horsemen carried pemmican in *parfleches,* rawhide packs strapped to their horses. Although pemmican was made by many other Native American groups in other areas, none relied on it quite as much as the people of the Plains.

Roll out pemmican between two sheets of wax paper.

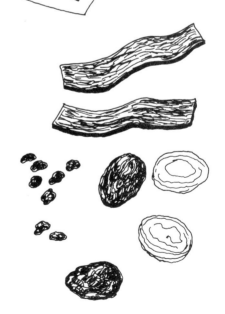

MATERIALS

2 ounces of dried beef jerky
Blender or food processor
Rubber spatula
4 dried apricot slices (or other dried fruit slices)
Handful of raisins, dried berries, or dried cherries
Wax paper
Rolling pin
Pie tin (optional)

DIRECTIONS

1. Grind the dried beef jerky in the blender until it is chopped very fine. Stop the blender from time to time to scrape the sides with the spatula.
2. Add the dried apricots and raisins or other dried fruit and grind these just as fine.
3. Empty the blender container onto a sheet of wax paper. Lay another sheet of wax paper on top so that the meat and fruit mixture is sandwiched in between. Then, roll over the top sheet with a rolling pin until the pemmican is flattened to about a 1/8-inch-thick pancake.
4. Let the pemmican dry between the wax paper sheets a day or two in the sun. Or dry it in an oven. Remove the pemmican from the wax paper by flipping it over into a pie tin. Set the tin in a 150° oven for 2 hours, turning the pemmican every once in a while as it dries.
5. Break off pieces to eat as a snack. Store leftover pemmican in a sealed container or plastic bag in the refrigerator.

Boiled Corn Cakes

Since it wasn't found growing wild, many Native Americans thought corn was first planted by the gods. The Iroquois believed a female spirit walked the earth once and took pity on the starving people. Cornstalks grew up everywhere she'd visited.

Corn was the most important food in Native American life. Many groups gave thanks for the plants at sowing and harvesting time. In the Southeast and Woodlands, people celebrated the ripening of the first ears in a "Green Corn Festival."

Among the Hopi, ripe corn was steamed in a fire pit and dried on the cob. As much as a 2-year supply might be stored away for those years when the rains didn't come. Hopi women ground dried kernels into cornmeal daily and prepared fried, baked, or boiled cornbread for every meal.

Drop 2 spoonsful of cornmeal mixture onto wet cornhusk.

MATERIALS

30 cornhusks, green or dried
1 or 2 cups of boiling water
Shallow pan, large enough to hold husks
    laid flat
3-quart pot, ¾ filled with water
1 cup of cornmeal flour
Quart bowl
Mixing spoon
½ cup honey
Blue food coloring (optional)
Slotted spoon
Knife or scissors

DIRECTIONS

1. Put the cornhusks in a pan and cover them with hot water.
2. Put a pot of water on the stove to boil.
3. Pour the cornmeal flour into the bowl.
4. Slowly mix 1 cup of boiling water into the cornmeal. Keep stirring the mixture. It should be the consistency of thick oatmeal. If it's too thick, add a little more boiling water and stir.
5. Stir in the honey.
6. Add 2 drops of blue food coloring if you want. The Hopi used blue cornmeal that made their cakes blue.

7. Open up one of the wet cornhusks. Drop 2 spoonfuls of the corn mixture into the center. Fold the sides of the husk over the mixture as shown. Fold the ends over one another to make a neat little packet.
8. Tear off a strip of another husk to use as string. Tie the husk packet together. Fill other husks and make more packets like this one.
9. Gently drop the packets into boiling water. Boil them 15 to 20 minutes. Lift them out with a slotted spoon. Cut the husk strings and open the packets. Sample the boiled corn cakes.

Fold ends over to make a neat packet.

Tear off strip from another husk and use as a string to tie up packet.

NATIVE AMERICAN GARDEN

The Iroquois believed that the spirits of three beautiful sisters lived in the fields and protected the crops. One sister guarded the corn plants; her hair was like the cornsilk. Another sister looked after the bean plants, and the third watched over the squash. The sisters were inseparable.

Like three close sisters, corn, bean, and squash seeds were planted together in one mound. The corn plants grew tall and straight, providing a pole for the bean vines to climb up and around. The squash plants sprawled at their feet. Most Native Americans grew these same three plants together in this way.

Native American farmers made gardening tools out of wood and bone. Digging sticks, which resembled stilts, were used like spades and shovels. A shoulder bone of a large animal was bound to a stick for a hoe, and a set of antlers attached in the same way made a rake. In the Southwest, a bucket of water and a gourd dipper were brought to the field for watering.

Little space is needed to plant a Native American garden. Hoe the soil and make small hills about 2 feet apart. Make several holes in the center of each mound about an inch deep. Drop in a few dried corn kernels, several beans, and some seeds from a squash, pumpkin, or gourd. You can do as Native Americans did and place a piece of raw fish in the mound. This is authentic Native American fertilizer. Or you can use manure or commercial fertilizer instead.

If there's space, don't limit the garden to the three sister plants. Grow some of the plants that were available to Native Americans in the wild. Plant green onions, a patch of strawberries, or a few sunflowers. Plant in the spring for an early fall harvest.

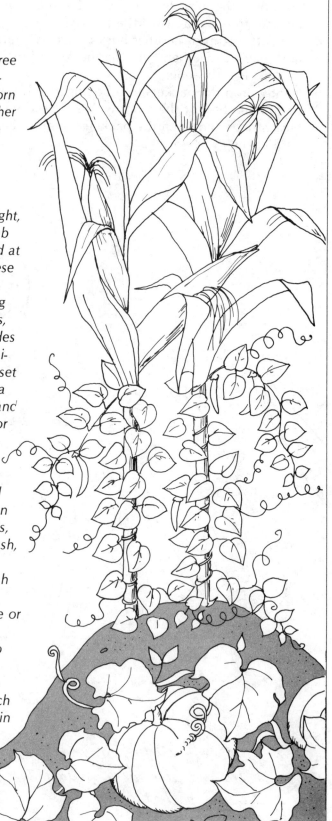

Wild Green Salad

Native Americans collected a large variety of wild greens that they ate raw, boiled like spinach, or fried. Some greens were served by themselves; others were cooked in with other foods for flavoring. All parts of a wild plant were eaten—the stems, leaves, and flowers. For example, the Plains people enjoyed both the blossoms and leaves of the wild nasturtium, which tastes much like radishes. They also ate raw or cooked wild onions and garlic, the greens as well as the bulbs. In the Southwest, young dandelion leaves were eaten raw. So were water cress, coriander, and mint leaves. California groups collected ferns, miner's lettuce, dill weed, mustard, and lamb's quarter.

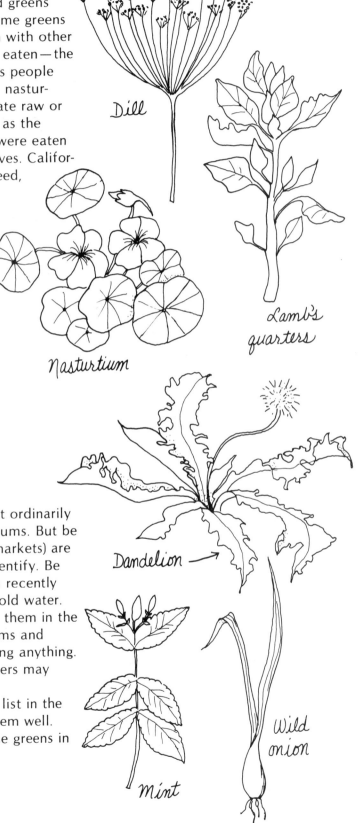

MATERIALS

Assortment of wild and cultivated greens collected out-of-doors, in a garden, or supermarket
Large bowl
¼ cup of vinegar
⅓ cup of sunflower or peanut oil
1 to 2 teaspoons of dill, chopped weed or seeds
1 tablespoon honey
Small bowl
Fork or wire whisk
Bowls and utensils

DIRECTIONS

1. Collect greens for a salad. Try to find ones not ordinarily eaten in salads, such as dandelions or nasturtiums. But be very careful. Some plants (not those in supermarkets) are poisonous. Only collect those that you can identify. Be sure the plants aren't in an area that has been recently sprayed with insecticide. Rinse the plants in cold water.
2. Tear the plant parts into small pieces and put them in the large bowl. Sample the various parts—the stems and flowers as well as the leaves—before discarding anything. Some parts may be tasteless or bitter, but others may taste fine.
3. Mix all the remaining food ingredients on the list in the small bowl. A fork or wire whisk will blend them well.
4. Pour the dressing from the small bowl over the greens in the large bowl. Toss the salad and serve it.

Nut Butter

Native Americans gathered harvests of nuts from hickory, beechnut, walnut, hazelnut, and butternut trees. These nuts were an important source of protein when meat was scarce. Since nuts stored so easily, they were kept to use when other foods were hard to come by. They were made into breads, soups, and pastes.

Nut and seed oils flavored many breads. The most common way nuts were eaten, however, was raw. During the winter, nuts were a treat passed around the fireside while old people told stories.

Gathering nuts and seeds in the fall was a joyful time for sharing work, food, talk, and games. Paiute families joined together to shake pine cones from pinon trees and roast the cones until the seeds popped out. The first night, everyone sang and gave thanks for the harvest. Then the cooks ground some pine nuts and made a soup for everyone to share.

Use tortilla or cracker to scoop nut butter from bowl.

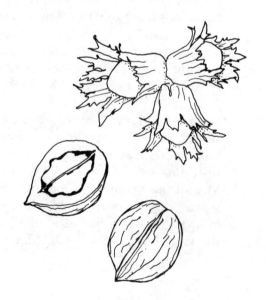

MATERIALS

1 cup of shelled nuts such as peanuts,
    pecans, beechnuts, hazelnuts, walnuts, or
    almonds
Blender or food processor
Small bowl and spoon, or mortar and pestle
1 to 3 tablespoons of sunflower or peanut oil
Honey
Tortillas, crackers, or bread
Knife

DIRECTIONS

1. Put the nuts in the blender and grind them into a fine powder.
2. Pour the nut flour into a bowl.
3. Add a little bit of oil at a time. Mix in oil until the nut butter is an easy-to-spread paste.
4. Taste it. Some nuts are sweeter than others. If you want to sweeten the butter, add a little bit of honey.
5. Use a tortilla as a spoon to scoop up some nut butter. Or spread the butter on crackers or bread.

Strawberry Juice

Native Americans used every part of the wild strawberry plant for food. They steeped the leaves in hot water to make a fragrant medicinal tea. They dried and ground the stems to make a powder for the skin. And they ate the fruit raw or dried, or they crushed it to remove the juice for a sweet, refreshing drink.

MATERIALS

12-ounce basket of ripe strawberries
Mortar and pestle, or bowl and wooden
   spoon
Bowl
2 cups of boiling water
Pitcher
Strainer
Honey
4 glasses with ice

Crush strawberries to a pulp.

DIRECTIONS

1. Remove stems and rinse the strawberries in cold water. Put them in the mortar and crush them to a pulp with the pestle, or mash them in a bowl with a wooden spoon.
2. Spoon the crushed berries into a bowl. Pour in 2 cups of boiling water and let the berries sit in the water for about a half hour.
3. Hold the strainer over the pitcher and pour in the berry and water mixture. When most of the liquid has gone into the pitcher, press the berries with the pestle to squeeze out the last juices. Then empty the strainer back into the bowl and save the strawberry pulp for a snack later.
4. Taste the strawberry juice. If the strawberries were very ripe, the juice will probably be sweet enough. Otherwise, add a teaspoon or two of honey.
5. Pour the juice into 4 glasses filled with ice. Serve it while it's cold.

Native American Celebration

In Native American life there were many small ceremonies that involved only a few people—a ceremony for naming a child, for example, or for working a healing prayer. But sometimes a whole village or several neighboring villages would come together for a large public celebration. These ceremonies were usually thanksgivings for an abundant harvest or a successful hunt. The changing of the seasons was also a time for public celebration. The gatherings lasted several days. They included many ritual offerings, prayers, and symbolic activities directed by priests or shamans. There were three important social aspects to a public ceremony—dancing, feasting, and playing games.

A class or a group of kids might want to organize a Native American celebration as an appropriate occasion to play native instruments, perform native dances, prepare native foods, display native crafts, and play native games.

Organize a Native American celebration around some important time, a holiday, or an event. Here are some suggestions:

- Harvest thanksgiving
- Winter solstice (on or near December 22)
- New Year
- First day of spring
- Last week of school
- Summer solstice (on or near June 22)
- A lunar or solar eclipse
- Native American Day (the fourth Friday in September)

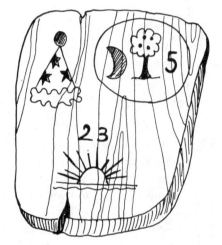

Be sure the celebration is in the spirit of an actual Native American ceremony, respectful of Native American culture. Don't merely imitate the dances and activities. The celebration should be a meaningful experience, an occasion to share and deepen understanding about Native American culture with friends.

If possible, write or talk with Native Americans who live nearby to learn more about particular dances or rituals. Also use the Resources on pages 91–92 for more detailed information.

INVITATIONS

Like the Algonquin, kids may want to send out invitations. The Algonquin delivered small pieces of wood decorated with picture writing to their guests.

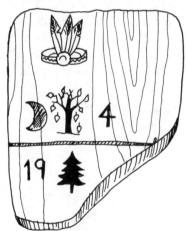

Invitations made from wood

CRAFTS DISPLAY

There are several ways to display Native American crafts. You can set up a Native American Museum. Clear some shelf or counter space to exhibit various crafts. Identify their purpose and the materials they're made from on labels. Another attractive way to display the more religious ceremonial objects is to "offer" them on an altar to the spirits that provided the materials. The Zuni "painted" an altar on the floor or ground with sand and filled it with offerings such as game equipment, food, animal effigies, and god's eyes.

You may also want to hold several crafts demonstrations. Show guests how to make a coiled basket or a clay coiled pot. Demonstrate how to make natural dyes and grind earth paints. Offer body paint to those without costumes, or fit them with decorated eye shades.

CEREMONIAL DANCE

Arrange for the performance of a ceremonial dance to celebrate the occasion. (See the Resources section at the end of this book for the names of books about Native American dances.) Kids may take part in circle or row dances, or may perform solo dances. Others may accompany them on their rhythmic instruments—clay pot water drums and gourd rattles. Recordings of Native American songs and dance music are available in the folk music sections of record stores or in the library. You may also order recordings through the mail order supply houses listed in the Resources on page 92.

A ceremonial dance offers the perfect opportunity to show off native costumes, such as a Jumping Dance headdress, kachina mask, cornhusk mask, Eskimo finger masks, ghost shirts, and feather fans. Use body paints and body ornaments as part of the costumes.

CEREMONIAL FEAST

Serve a selection of Native American foods in a buffet. Allow guests to sample dried fruits, pemmican, boiled corn cakes, wild greens, nut butter, and strawberry juice. Offer thanks to the Earth Mother.

NATIVE AMERICAN GAMES

Set up a gaming corner on a large blanket. Teach guests to play basket gamble, hidden ball, and harpoon the seal. Play games like jackrabbits hit, corncob darts, and ring and pin toss in an area where there is more room. For team games, such as kick-stick race, find out everybody's birthdays. Those born in the winter are the ptarmigans; those born in summer are the sea pigeons; those born in "freeze" or "break- up" (fall or spring) can play on either side.

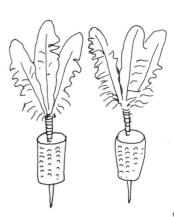

Native American Designs and Colors

Native Americans decorated most of their crafts to make them more beautiful. They added color and designs with paint, beads, quill embroidery, and by carving and weaving. Sometimes a design or color was a symbol, that is, it stood for an idea or told a story. For example, among the Crow, the color black was a symbol for victory; arrow symbols might mean a hunt or a battle.

Each group had its own set of meanings for colors and designs to use on ceremonial crafts. These symbols could be drawn on a leather pouch or a drumskin to retell a myth or relate an important event. Sometimes the maker of a ghost shirt or some other ceremonial object had a dream that revealed what design to use. Designs that came in dreams had special supernatural powers.

The decorative art on many everyday objects had no special meaning. Sometimes a geometric design might be called "butterfly" because the triangle shapes together on a basket looked like a butterfly. Usually, the only way to find out if a design was supposed to be a symbol with meaning was to ask the maker. Designs that showed people, birds, and animals were usually created by men. Women worked more with geometric shapes.

Color was important to add meaning to a design, too. Most Native Americans named four points of the earth, the four directions of the compass—north, south, east, and west—and assigned a color to each one. Among the Cherokee, north was blue, south was white, east was red, and west was black. Colors could also mean life or death, war or peace, female or male, night or day. For example, the Navaho thought black represented men and blue, women. The Hopi thought that the color blue was the most sacred and used it to honor their gods. Here are some of the other meanings attached to colors:

Color	Meaning for Native Americans
Black	night, underworld, male, cold, disease, death
Blue	sky, water, female, clouds, lightning, moon, thunder, sadness
Green	plant life, earth, summer, rain
Red	wounds, sunset, thunder, blood, earth, war, day
White	winter, death, snow
Yellow	sunshine, day, dawn

woven sash

Choose a color and write down all the thoughts, feelings, or ideas it brings to mind. Do this for several colors and give a meaning to each color. Select a color to represent each of the four directions, north, south, east, and west. Consider these meanings when planning a design.

Important events in the life of a Native American person or group were sometimes recorded on rawhide or birch bark using picture writing. To tell a story with a design, use simple pictures to suggest the events. For example, a sun, a person, and a bicycle on a blue background might record a bike riding adventure to a lake. Some important events that were printed in pictures included the killing of the first bear, the birth of a baby brother, a heavy snowfall, curing of a serious illness, a good corn crop, and a meteor shower.

Combine some of the design elements here to decorate your own crafts. Be imaginative and put some of your own spirit into each design.

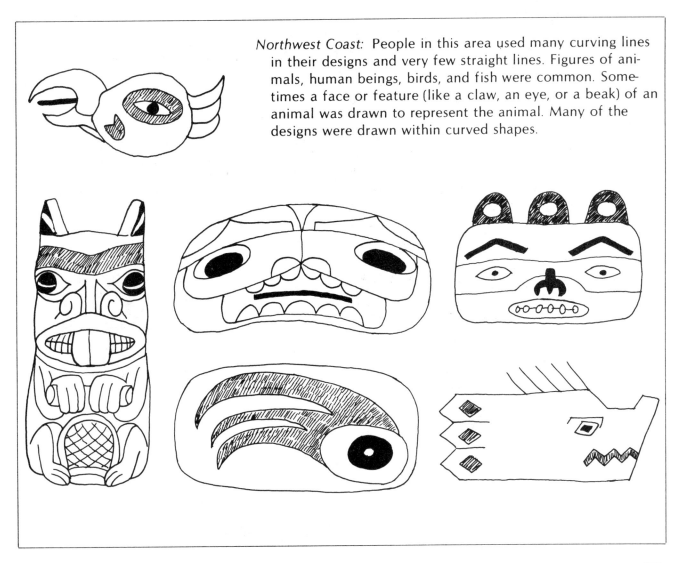

Northwest Coast: People in this area used many curving lines in their designs and very few straight lines. Figures of animals, human beings, birds, and fish were common. Sometimes a face or feature (like a claw, an eye, or a beak) of an animal was drawn to represent the animal. Many of the designs were drawn within curved shapes.

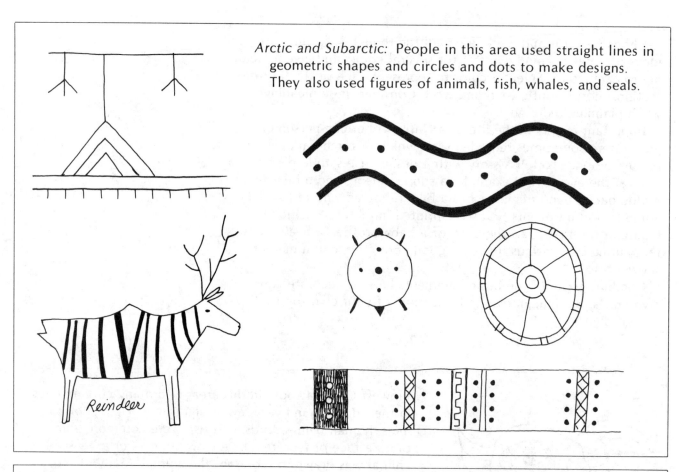

Arctic and Subarctic: People in this area used straight lines in geometric shapes and circles and dots to make designs. They also used figures of animals, fish, whales, and seals.

Reindeer

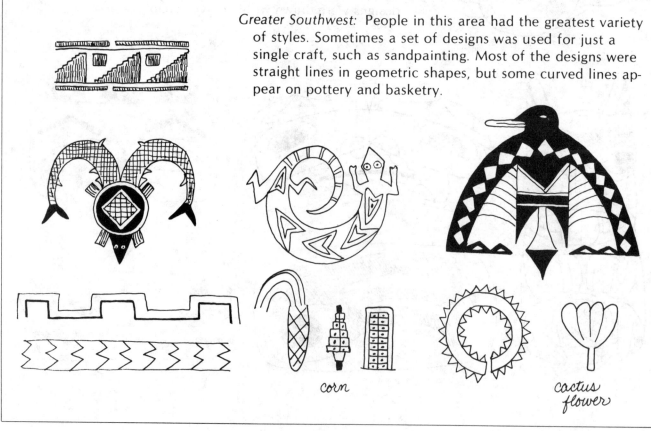

Greater Southwest: People in this area had the greatest variety of styles. Sometimes a set of designs was used for just a single craft, such as sandpainting. Most of the designs were straight lines in geometric shapes, but some curved lines appear on pottery and basketry.

corn

cactus flower

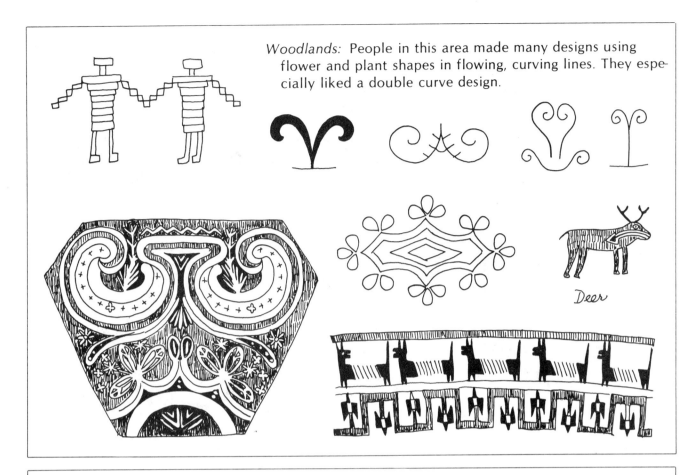

Woodlands: People in this area made many designs using flower and plant shapes in flowing, curving lines. They especially liked a double curve design.

Deer

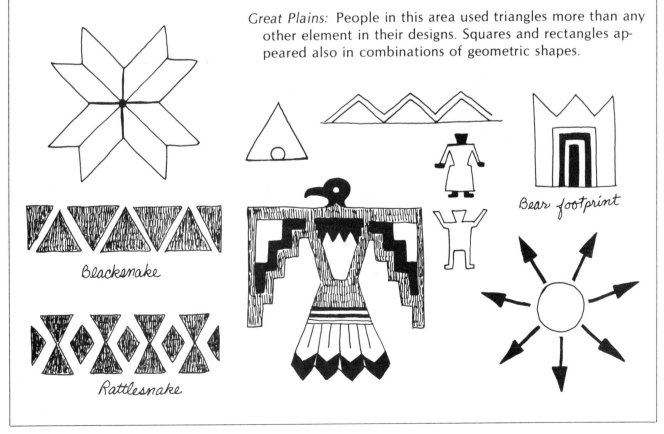

Great Plains: People in this area used triangles more than any other element in their designs. Squares and rectangles appeared also in combinations of geometric shapes.

Blacksnake

Rattlesnake

Bear footprint

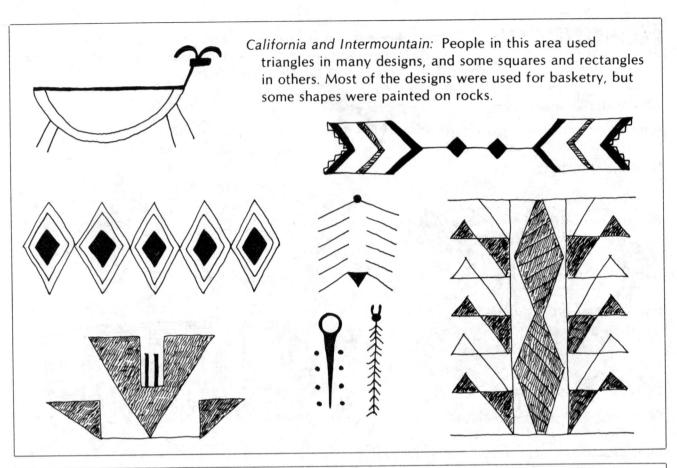

California and Intermountain: People in this area used triangles in many designs, and some squares and rectangles in others. Most of the designs were used for basketry, but some shapes were painted on rocks.

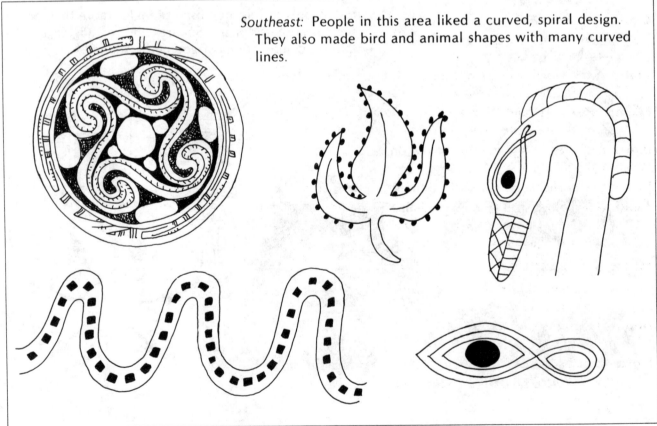

Southeast: People in this area liked a curved, spiral design. They also made bird and animal shapes with many curved lines.

Resources

GENERAL INFORMATION

America's Fascinating Indian Heritage. Maxwell, James A., editor. New York: Reader's Digest Association, 1978.

Indian Leaflet Series. Douglas, Frederic H., editor. Denver Art Museum, n.d. (For a list of titles, write: Denver Art Museum, 1300 Logan Street, Denver, CO 80203.)

Ishi in Two Worlds: A Biography of the Last Wild Indian in North America. Kroeber, Theodora. Berkeley: University of California Press, 1961.

Native Americans, The. Spencer, Robert F., et al. New York: Harper & Row, Publishers, 1965.

Weewish Tree, The: A Magazine of Indian America for Young People. (For subscription information, write to: American Indian Historical Society, 1451 Masonic Avenue, San Francisco, CA 94117.)

CRAFTS

American Indian Craft Book, The. Minor, Marz Nono. New York: Popular Library, 1972.

Book of Indian Crafts and Costumes. Mason, Bernard S. New York: The Ronald Press Company, 1946.

Crafts from North American Indian Arts: Techniques, Designs, and Contemporary Applications. Stribling, Mary Lou. New York: Crown Publishers, 1975.

Crafts of the North American Indians: A Craftsman's Manual. Schneider, Richard C. New York: Van Nostrand Reinhold, 1972.

Eskimo Masks: Art and Ceremony. Ray, Dorothy Jean. Seattle: University of Washington Press, 1967.

Indian Basketry. James, George Wharton. New York: Dover Publications, 1972.

Indian Crafts and Lore. Hunt, W. Ben. New York: Golden Press, 1954.

Tapestries in Sand: The Spirit of Indian Sandpainting. Villaseñor, David. Healdsburg, CA: The Naturegraph Company, 1966.

MUSIC

American Indians and Their Music, The. Densmore, Francis. New York: The Womans Press, 1926.

Drums, Tomtoms, and Rattles. Mason, Bernard S. New York: Dover Publications, 1974.

Indian Dances of North America: Their Importance to Indian Life. Laubin, Reginald and Gladys. Norman, OK: University of Oklahoma Press, 1977.

GAMES

Eskimo Inuit Games. Eger, F. H., compiler. Montreal, Quebec: X-Press, 1900. (To order, write: X-Press, 519 de Gaspe, Suite 212, Nuns' Island, Montreal, Quebec H3E 1E9. It is also available in some museum bookstores.)

Games of the American Indian. Baldwin, Gordon C. New York: W. W. Norton and Company, 1969.

Games of the North American Indians. Culin, Stewart. New York: Dover Publications, 1975.

FOOD

Art of American Indian Cooking, The. Kimball, Yeffe, and Jean Anderson. New York: Doubleday and Company and McIntosh and Otis, 1965.

Foods the Indians Gave Us. Hays, Wilma P. and R. Vernon. New York: Ives Washburn, 1973.

Hopi Cookery. Kavena, Juanita Tiger. Tucson: University of Arizona Press, 1980.

Native Harvests: Recipes and Botanicals of the American Indian. Barrie Kavasch. New York: Random House, 1979.

MAIL ORDER SUPPLY HOUSES

Grey Owl Indian Craft Manufacturing Co., 150-02 Beaver Road, Jamaica, NY 11433. Send $1 for catalog of kits and supplies.

Plume Trading and Sales Co., Inc., P.O. Box 585, Monroe, NY 10950. Send 50¢ for catalog of kits, books, and records.

Supernaw's Oklahoma Indian Supply, 301 East WC Rogers Boulevard, Skiatook, OK 74070. Send $1 for catalog of supplies.